THE

MELCHIZEDEK

PRIESTHOOD

THE

MELCHIZEDEK

PRIESTHOOD

Understanding the
DOCTRINE

Living the
PRINCIPLES

DALE G. RENLUND
RUTH LYBBERT RENLUND

DESERET
BOOK

SALT LAKE CITY, UTAH

Library of Congress Cataloging-in-Publication Data

Names: Renlund, Dale G., 1952– author. | Renlund, Ruth Lybbert, 1954– author.

Title: The Melchizedek Priesthood: understanding the doctrine, living the principles / Dale G. Renlund, Ruth Lybbert Renlund.

Description: Salt Lake City, Utah : Deseret Book, [2018] | Includes bibliographical references and index.

Identifiers: LCCN 2017051989 | ISBN 9781629724454 (hardbound : alk. paper)

Subjects: LCSH: Melchizedek Priesthood (Mormon Church) | Mormon Church—Doctrines. | The Church of Jesus Christ of Latter-day Saints—Doctrines.

Classification: LCC BX8659.6 .R46 2018 | DDC 262/.1493—dc23

LC record available at https://lccn.loc.gov/2017051989

Printed in the United States of America
Publishers Printing, Salt Lake City, UT

10 9 8 7 6 5 4 3 2 1

To the finest priesthood holders we have known, our fathers.

MERLIN R. LYBBERT
(January 31, 1926–July 6, 2001)

MATS ÅKE RENLUND
(September 25, 1917–December 4, 2009)

CONTENTS

PREFACE

Our Heavenly Father's power is both awesome and delicate. It is awesome because it is all-encompassing, omnipotent, and omniscient. It is delicate because its use is carefully controlled by eternal laws and principles. Yet, He gives some of His power to individuals who He knows perfectly well are imperfect. How does it work? How is it conceivable that His awesome, delicate power could be used by both an illiterate farmer and a rocket scientist—to equal effect—in the salvation of humankind? This book attempts to address such questions.

To help His children use and benefit from the priesthood, God has provided a set of principles that govern its use. This set of principles is a portion of what is referred to as the doctrine of the priesthood. *Doctrine* in this context is used in the same way that *military doctrine* refers to guidelines, standard operating procedures, or rules of engagement for military personnel.

The book is divided into two sections: the first discusses the foundations of the doctrine of the priesthood, and the second discusses the principles themselves. Our hope is that the book makes it possible for both men and women to understand the priesthood better. The book is not an exhaustive reference source for everything priesthood-related in the scriptures, nor is it a compendium of every authoritative statement on the topic. Rather, we seek to consider questions about the priesthood in a simple, straightforward manner.

We have made a conscious decision to direct the contents of this book primarily to those who hold the Melchizedek Priesthood and those who are preparing to receive it. However, it is not our intent to exclude women from the discussion. The reason both our names appear on the book's cover is because the conclusions we have drawn about priesthood principles and practices are the result of our joint study and discussions over the years. The priesthood deeply affects all Heavenly Father's children, male and female, and both men and women need to understand it. We hope this book will be a helpful resource that will generate further thought, conversation, and understanding.

Preparing to receive the Melchizedek Priesthood can occur in many ways. President Thomas S. Monson relates an experience wherein he learned about the priesthood from his stake president. President Monson recalls:

> As I approached my 18th birthday and prepared to enter the mandatory military service required of young men during World War II, I was recommended to receive the Melchizedek Priesthood, but first I needed to telephone my stake president, Paul C. Child, for an interview. . . . Having heard from some of my friends of his rather detailed and searching interviews,

I desired minimum exposure of my scriptural knowledge; therefore, when I called him I suggested we meet the following Sunday at a time I knew was just an hour before his sacrament meeting time.

His response: "Oh, Brother Monson, that would not provide us sufficient time to peruse the scriptures." He then suggested a time three hours before his sacrament meeting, and he instructed me to bring with me my personally marked and referenced set of scriptures.

When I arrived at his home on Sunday, I was greeted warmly, and then the interview began. President Child said, "Brother Monson, you hold the Aaronic Priesthood. Have you ever had angels minister to you?" I replied that I had not. When he asked if I knew I was entitled to such, I again replied that I had not known.

He instructed, "Brother Monson, repeat from memory the 13th section of the Doctrine and Covenants."

I began, "Upon you my fellow servants, in the name of Messiah I confer the Priesthood of Aaron, which holds the keys of the ministering of angels—"

"Stop," President Child directed. Then, in a calm, kindly tone, he counseled, "Brother Monson, never forget that as a holder of the Aaronic Priesthood you are entitled to the ministering of angels."

It was almost as though an angel were in the room that day. I have never forgotten the interview. I yet feel the spirit of that solemn occasion as we together read of the responsibilities, the duties, and the blessings of the Aaronic Priesthood and the Melchizedek Priesthood—blessings which come not only to us but also to our families and to others we will have the privilege to serve.[1]

Not all of us will be blessed to have a stake president like President Paul C. Child who takes the time and makes the effort to review the responsibilities, duties, and blessings of the priesthood with each prospective elder. This book seeks to provide a platform for such discussions and learning.

Additionally, the book has arisen in large part from questions we have asked each other over the years. These questions have led to study, observation, and discussion. The quest for an understanding of the priesthood and its proper application has continued through our respective medical and legal training and our careers outside of the home. A fuller understanding and application of priesthood power has required both of us to work together inside our home. A major augmentation in our learning occurred as our amazing daughter, Ashley Ruth Renlund, joined our family. From an early age, her fresh questions, clear insights, and intolerance for "fuzzy" thinking have refined the process.

We have chosen to write this book in the first-person-plural voice unless the event that we wish to relate is specific to Elder Renlund. In that case, we have written in the first-person-singular voice. Even in those instances, Sister Renlund's authorship contribution has been significant.

Many have provided helpful comments and suggestions to us as the book developed. We especially wish to thank Anita M. Renlund, Gary M. Renlund, Roger G. Clarke, Richard L. Curtis, Linda C. R. Maurer, Paul J. Dirkmaat, and Ashley R. Renlund. We appreciate the time they have taken to read and discuss the book. Our editor from Deseret Book, Emily Watts, has been extraordinarily helpful from the outset and throughout the process.

In this book, we express our views and opinions, based on our own experience and learning. We wish to make it clear that these opinions and views are ours; we alone are responsible for them.

This is *not* a publication of The Church of Jesus Christ of Latter-day Saints. No part of this book has been written under assignment of or at the request of the First Presidency or the Quorum of the Twelve Apostles. Therefore, the views expressed in this book cannot and do not represent the official position of The Church of Jesus Christ of Latter-day Saints.

NOTE

1. Thomas S. Monson, "The Priesthood—A Sacred Gift," *Ensign,* May 2015.

FOUNDATIONS AND DOCTRINE OF THE PRIESTHOOD

The doctrine of the priesthood shall
distil upon thy soul as the dews from heaven.
—DOCTRINE AND COVENANTS 121:45

Imagine that man is given a special piano when he is ordained to the priesthood. The musical output from the piano represents priesthood power. Consider that the piano keys sense both conferred priesthood authority and righteousness. Righteousness is not synonymous with perfection, but the term implies that the priesthood holder is making every reasonable effort to be worthy of the priesthood he holds. If the piano keys sense both the man's conferred authority and his righteousness, the depression of a key is coupled with a hammer that hits a string and produces a musical note. If either conferred authority or righteousness is missing, the key strike is uncoupled from the hammer, and no sound results.

When a priesthood holder is first issued his special piano, he is not able to play a piano concerto. In fact, his authority is restricted to only some keys, such as the middle register. Later, as he receives more priesthood authority, more piano keys become available to him, until he has access to the entire keyboard. Regardless of how many keys he is authorized to play, initially, the music is simplistic and occasionally cacophonic. But as he continues practicing over and over, the music improves. Eventually, the result is a piano concerto.

Like the imaginary piano, the powers of heaven are delicate. To be effective in gaining access to them, we need to learn and apply a set of principles that govern the use of Heavenly Father's delegated power. In other words, it takes practice and self-control to be a world-class priesthood holder. God does not expect a priesthood holder to play piano concertos right away or even to understand how the special piano works. But He does expect a priesthood holder to exercise the priesthood he has been given and over time become adept at handling that power. This process involves understanding the doctrine of the priesthood. As the priesthood holder uses his priesthood authority and power, he comes to understand the doctrine of the priesthood. During the time of learning, our Father will make the priesthood holder's exercise of priesthood power adequate for the task at hand.

The doctrine of the priesthood, referred to in Doctrine and Covenants 121:45, includes a revealed set of principles governing the use of the priesthood. As one exercises priesthood authority, these principles become more and more natural. Over time, using these principles, a priesthood holder behaves more like the Savior and becomes more trustworthy in using the priesthood.

A foundation for understanding priesthood must be built before discussing the doctrine of the priesthood.[1] Therefore, the first section of this book addresses these fundamental questions:

- What is the priesthood?[2]
- What is the purpose of the priesthood?

- What are priesthood offices and keys?
- What are oaths and covenants generally, and what are the oaths and covenants that are specifically associated with the priesthood?
- What are the commandments associated with the oath and covenant of the priesthood?

The second part of the book discusses the doctrine of the priesthood, or the set of principles governing the use of the priesthood. These principles derive from a revelation to Joseph Smith in 1839 recorded as Doctrine and Covenants, section 121. The Lord states that many are called to His work but few are chosen because they do not learn this one lesson: "That the rights of the priesthood are inseparably connected with the powers of heaven, and that the powers of heaven cannot be controlled nor handled only upon the principles of righteousness" (Doctrine and Covenants 121:36).

This should come as no surprise. Priesthood is God's power, a portion of which is delegated to man, for the salvation and exaltation of Heavenly Father's children. To use God's power, the priesthood holder must be worthy, align his will to God's, act in faith, and function in accord with His established principles.

Some of these principles are explicitly stated in the revelation (Doctrine and Covenants 121), including:

- Impairment of priesthood authority occurs when "we undertake to cover our sins, or to gratify our pride, our vain ambition, or to exercise control or dominion or compulsion . . . in any degree of unrighteousness" (verse 37).
- The proper exercise of priesthood authority must be learned. Few naturally act properly because "it is the nature and disposition of almost all men, as soon as they get a little authority . . . they will immediately begin to exercise unrighteous dominion" (verse 39).

- The proper exercise of priesthood power or influence is maintained only by "persuasion, by long-suffering, by gentleness and meekness, and by love unfeigned; by kindness, and pure knowledge" (verses 41–42). Force is out of the question. Only Christlike attributes are used in its exercise. Proper priesthood influence is dependent on the agency of those upon whom and for whom the priesthood is exercised.
- Only the Holy Ghost should prompt and authorize a priesthood holder to reprove or chasten another, and then only with clarity and focus. Thereafter, the priesthood holder must clearly demonstrate that the main reason for the correction is love of the individual (verse 43).

In addition to these explicitly stated principles, the Lord also makes it clear that the prime motivation for the priesthood holder in his exercise of priesthood must be charity, or the pure love of Christ (see Moroni 7:47–48). So, in addition to understanding the connection between the rights of the priesthood and principles of righteousness, the Lord exhorts the priesthood holder to be motivated by charity. He says:

"Let thy bowels *also* be full of charity towards all men, and to the household of faith, and let virtue garnish thy thoughts unceasingly; then shall thy confidence wax strong in the presence of God; and the doctrine of the priesthood shall distil upon thy soul as the dews from heaven" (Doctrine and Covenants 121:45; emphasis added).

The promised blessings that come from exercising priesthood authority in this way are explicitly stated: the priesthood holder's confidence will wax strong in the presence of God, and the doctrine of the priesthood will distill on his soul. The priesthood holder can be confident in the presence of God because he behaves more like Christ; he is more dependable and predictable. Heavenly Father can begin to trust him as He trusts Christ Himself. Nephi, the son of Helaman and the brother of Lehi, was such a priesthood holder. Christ said to him:

> Blessed art thou, Nephi, for those things which thou hast done; for I have beheld how thou hast with unwearyingness declared the word, which I have given unto thee, unto this people. And thou hast not feared them, and hast not sought thine own life, but hast sought my will, and to keep my commandments.
>
> And now, because thou hast done this with such unwearyingness, behold, I will bless thee forever; and I will make thee mighty in word and in deed, in faith and in works; yea, even that all things shall be done unto thee according to thy word, *for thou shalt not ask that which is contrary to my will.* (Helaman 10:4–5; emphasis added)

Nephi qualified for the blessing of having confidence in the presence of God because he demonstrated consistently that his will was aligned with God's and that he would not ask for anything that was contrary to God's will. This did not happen at the beginning of Nephi's ministry, but after Nephi was tested and tried and had demonstrated his worthiness.

This pathway toward gaining the confidence of God is the key that unlocks the meaning of the doctrine of the priesthood *distilling* upon one's soul as the dews from heaven. In what way would principles governing the use of the priesthood distill on the soul? Why would the Lord use the term *distill* to characterize the process?

Distillation is a method of separating mixtures based on differences in the volatility of the components in a boiling liquid mixture. Distillation is not a chemical reaction; rather, it is a physical separation of compounds. It is used to increase the purity of a desired component. For instance, water is distilled to remove impurities.

Distillation of fermented solutions has been done since ancient times to produce distilled beverages with a higher alcohol content.

Applying the concept of distillation to the doctrine of the priesthood suggests that in exercising priesthood authority in the proper way, a man incorporates Christlike attributes into his soul, pure and simple. The impurity that melts away is the "natural-man" tendency inherent in every priesthood holder. His tendency to act contrary to the doctrine of the priesthood is supplanted by pure motives and righteous conduct. In this way, the dews from heaven come drop by drop into his life.

As a priesthood holder exercises priesthood authority in the right way, those aspects of his life that naturally seek to maintain authority without regard to the powers of heaven are discarded. Those parts of his nature that seek to use authority for personal gain are discarded. Those parts of his nature that seek to use force, guilt, or intimidation are discarded. Over time, all that is left of his soul are Christlike attributes that allow him to naturally use the priesthood in the proper way.

For this set of principles to be incorporated into one's soul, the priesthood must be used. The exercise of priesthood authority is the "heat" that distills the priesthood holder's soul. He will not naturally understand these principles by reading a book or theorizing about them in a class or seminary but by practicing them. When the doctrine of the priesthood has been incorporated into spiritual DNA, when it has distilled on the soul as dews from heaven, then this blessing comes: "The Holy Ghost shall be thy constant companion, and thy scepter an unchanging scepter of righteousness and truth; and thy dominion shall be an everlasting dominion, and without *compulsory* means it shall flow unto thee forever and ever" (Doctrine and Covenants 121:46, emphasis added).

When the blessings flow "without compulsory means," the

proper exercise of priesthood authority becomes natural. God's authority is used in God's way. Thought of in this way, the doctrine of the priesthood is not a grand, unifying doctrine that is unknown to most. It is not mysterious, unknown to all but the most experienced and righteous, or reserved only to those in the leading councils of the Church.[3] The doctrine of the priesthood is simple. It informs the priesthood holder how the priesthood is to be used. We need not assume that the principles discussed are the only ones that constitute the doctrine of the priesthood. But the principles taught in the following chapters will assist a priesthood holder to increase his confidence before God and become a natural priesthood holder, becoming like our Father.

NOTES

1. *Definitions of the priesthood.* There is no difficulty in finding definitions for the priesthood. The Guide to the Scriptures indicates that the priesthood is "the authority and power that God gives to man to act in all things for the salvation of man (Doctrine and Covenants 50:26–27)." The priesthood is God's authority and power. It is given to men on earth to implement Heavenly Father's plan for the salvation and exaltation of His children.

   Joseph Smith defined priesthood as "an everlasting principle" (*Teachings of the Prophet Joseph Smith,* comp. Joseph Fielding Smith [1976], 157) and as a "law of theocracy" (ibid., 322).

2. *The doctrine of the priesthood.* According to the *Oxford English Dictionary,* the first use of the word *doctrine* was in the twelfth century in vernacular French and in Latin. The meaning of *doctrine* has evolved over time, ranging from a piece of instruction, a lesson, or precept; a body of instruction or teaching, a belief, theoretical opinion; a dogma, tenet. *Doctrine* in the eighteenth and nineteenth centuries could be applied to political and religious ideas—for example, the doctrine of the equality of all men, the Monroe doctrine, and the doctrine of the sacred Trinity. A definition of the word that might be most applicable to its use in Doctrine and Covenants 121:45 is "a body or system of principles or tenets."

3. Elder Bruce R. McConkie taught, "This doctrine of the priesthood— unknown in the world and but little known even in the Church—cannot be learned out of the scriptures alone. It is not set forth in the sermons and teachings of the prophets and Apostles, except in small measure. The doctrine of the priesthood is known only by personal revelation. It comes, line upon line and precept upon precept, by the power of the Holy Ghost

to those who love and serve God with all their heart, might, mind, and strength" ("The Doctrine of the Priesthood," *Ensign,* May 1982). The assertion made in this book is to the contrary. Rather than being little known in the Church, the doctrine of the priesthood is known. It has been revealed in scripture. Apostles and prophets have taught and continue to teach it. It is the set of principles that govern the use of the priesthood. The practical application is what must be learned through revelation, as the doctrine must be experienced to help us become like God.

FOUNDATIONS

of the

PRIESTHOOD

Chapter 1

THE PRIESTHOOD

*Thus they become high priests forever, after the order
of the Son, the Only Begotten of the Father.*

—ALMA 13:6–9

The concept of priesthood in The Church of Jesus Christ of
Latter-day Saints is unique and perhaps confusing for those
who are unfamiliar with it. Even many members of the Church
who accept, love, and appreciate the priesthood may find themselves
"fuzzy" on the doctrine and principles. Perhaps that is because the
term *priesthood* is used in at least two ways. First, *priesthood* is the
term used to describe the total power and authority of God. Second,
priesthood is also the term used to describe the power and authority
that God gives to ordained priesthood holders on earth to act in all
things necessary for the salvation of God's children.[1] This second usage is the widely accepted definition of the priesthood. For example,
Preach My Gospel defines *priesthood* as the authority and power that
God gives to man to act in the name of Jesus Christ in all things for
the salvation of mankind.[2] Thus, the same word, *priesthood,* refers

both to God's total power and authority and to that portion of His power and authority that He delegates to man on earth.

Linguistically, some terms can be used to refer to a larger whole as well as to a part. Consider the term *earth,* which can mean both the planet on which we reside and the topsoil we push around in gardens. Certainly, the planet Earth encompasses garden topsoil, but garden topsoil does not encompass the planet Earth. Context usually makes the meaning clear.

Similarly, context usually makes the meaning of the word *priesthood* clear. However, misunderstandings can arise when people in and out of the Church equate priesthood ordination with the total priesthood power and authority of God.

God holds unlimited, unbounded, and unending power and authority. He has delegated some of His authority and power to ordained priesthood holders on earth—specifically, that which is necessary to bring about the salvation of mankind. The offices of the Aaronic and Melchizedek Priesthood do not constitute all of God's priesthood, His total power and authority. Brigham Young taught that there are many aspects of God's total priesthood power and authority that are not delegated to men on earth. He said:

> It is supposed . . . that we have all the ordinances in our possession for life and salvation, and exaltation, and that we are administering in those ordinances. This is not the case. We are in possession of all the ordinances that can be administered in the flesh; but there are other ordinances and administrations that must be administered beyond this world. I know you would like to ask what they are. I will mention one. We have not, neither can we receive here, the ordinance and the keys of resurrection. . . . This is one of the ordinances we can not receive here [on the earth], and there are many more.[3]

Indeed, we may wish that Brother Brigham mentioned other things besides the keys of resurrection. He does, however, allude to other authority and power retained by God—the authority and power to produce bodies *and* spirits, create kingdoms, and organize matter. Referring to these statements by Brigham Young, President Spencer W. Kimball said that "we talk about the gospel in its fulness; yet we realize that a large part is still available to us as we prepare, as we perfect our lives, and as we become more like our God."[4]

We must, therefore, recognize that God has conferred only a portion of His total priesthood power and authority. This concept is illustrated graphically in Figure 1, which demonstrates the relationship between God's total priesthood power and authority and that portion of His power and authority that He has delegated to man on earth through priesthood ordination.

Consider that God's total priesthood power and authority is

Figure 1.

represented by the entire sphere, both the spherical segment or cone and the remainder of the sphere, with the radius of the sphere being infinite. God delegates and confers a portion of His authority and power to ordained priesthood holders on earth, represented as the cone. Since the radius of the sphere is infinite, the volume of the power and authority represented by the cone is also infinite.

All blessings come from God's total priesthood power and authority. Priesthood power and blessings, by that expanded definition, have been and always will be available to all who qualify for them, without restriction based on gender, birth order, or lineage. This principle can readily be seen from multiple examples in which God's power was manifest at a time when conferred priesthood did not exist on the earth. Many spiritual and devoted individuals complied with laws that govern reception of God's blessings, without having received any priesthood ordination. Christian reformers such as William Tyndale, Martin Luther, and John Calvin received God's power as they translated the Bible and participated in other inspired activities.

Even after the Great Apostasy, God was not "snoozing" until the priesthood was conferred on Joseph Smith and Oliver Cowdery on May 15, 1829 (Doctrine and Covenants 13).[5] Before and after the Reformation, God blessed men and women, Protestants, Catholics, and non-Christians by His priesthood power and authority as they prayed and lived according to the light and knowledge they received.

Joseph Smith originally accessed God's priesthood power and authority without priesthood keys and without conferred priesthood authority. God the Father and Jesus Christ appeared to Joseph Smith after his sincere prayer before priesthood keys had been restored to the earth. The Book of Mormon was translated in part *by the gift and power of God* before Joseph Smith received any priesthood ordination. What power, then, did Joseph Smith have access to? The only answer is God's priesthood power and authority.

The same is true today, although the keys of the priesthood are on the earth. People who are not members of the Church or who do not hold conferred priesthood pray and receive answers, exercise faith, and are healed. Those who live God's commandments are blessed.

Through revelation, there is much we know about the power and authority God has delegated to men through priesthood ordination.[6] We know that priesthood keys must necessarily function within the context of God's total priesthood power and authority. All priesthood keys for the earth are held by Jesus Christ, and the priesthood conferred upon mortal men was anciently named after Him: the Holy Priesthood, after the order of the Son of God (Doctrine and Covenants 107:2–3). This is why ordained holders of the priesthood act in the name of Jesus Christ. In this role, a priesthood holder performs ordinances that will be recognized by God as valid. Conferred priesthood authority also includes the right and responsibility to preside within the organizational structure of the Church. Through priesthood keys, God governs His Church. By conferred priesthood authority, the gospel is preached and the ordinances of salvation and exaltation for both the living and the dead are performed.

Priesthood is the conduit for obtaining revelation in the Church, the channel through which God reveals Himself and His glory, His intents and His purposes. Although men and women both receive revelation through God's priesthood power for their specific stewardships and responsibilities, the Melchizedek Priesthood holds "the key of the mysteries of the kingdom, even the key of the knowledge of God" (Doctrine and Covenants 84:19–20).[7] Through those who hold priesthood keys, the mind and will of God for His people as a whole are conveyed. When priesthood is employed by His servants on His errand, it functions as if by the Lord's own mouth and hand (Doctrine and Covenants 1:38).

But there are still many things we do not know about priesthood power and authority. For example, why does God restrict His delegation of power and authority? Today only fifteen men have received all priesthood authority and keys, and only one on earth, the President of the Church is authorized to direct the use of those keys in their entirety.

In fact, there has never been a time in the history of the earth when priesthood ordination has not been restricted to specific individuals, groups, or tribes. It has never been given to all of God's children.

In ancient Israel, firstborn males were hallowed to the Lord at the time of the Exodus (see Numbers 3:13). Later, those of the tribe of Levi were substituted for these firstborn males, to have charge of the whole congregation before the tabernacle and to do the service of the tabernacle. Aaron and his sons were designated the priests that officiated in the tabernacle (see Numbers 3). Non-Levites could not be priests or even hold the Levitical Priesthood.

After the Babylonian captivity, the children of priests whose genealogies were lost were denied priesthood ordination (see Ezra 2). It is reasonable to suppose that they were just as worthy as those who could prove their genealogy, yet they were prevented from officiating as priests. How can this disparate treatment be reconciled? We really do not have a complete understanding. However, it is important to remember that while the tribe of Levi and the descendants of Aaron were the ones ordained to the priesthood, all of Israel benefitted equally from the ordinances God prescribed.

For a time in this dispensation, black men of African ancestry were not permitted to be ordained to the priesthood. Why? The Church offers this statement on the matter:

The gospel of Jesus Christ is for everyone. The Book of Mormon states, "black and white, bond and free, male and female; . . . all are alike unto God" (2 Nephi 26:33). This is the Church's official teaching.

People of all races have always been welcomed and baptized into the Church since its beginning. In fact, by the end of his life in 1844 Joseph Smith, the founding prophet of The Church of Jesus Christ of Latter-day Saints, opposed slavery. During this time some black males were ordained to the priesthood. At some point the Church stopped ordaining male members of African descent, although there were a few exceptions. It is not known precisely why, how or when this restriction began in the Church, but it has ended. Church leaders sought divine guidance regarding the issue and more than three decades ago extended the priesthood to all worthy male members. The Church immediately began ordaining members to priesthood offices wherever they attended throughout the world.[8]

Recently the Church also made the following statement on this subject: "The origins of priesthood availability are not entirely clear. Some explanations with respect to this matter were made in the absence of direct revelation and references to these explanations are sometimes cited in publications. These previous personal statements do not represent Church doctrine."[9]

Importantly, Heavenly Father through the priesthood offers His eternal promises to each of His children. All have equal access in the end to His love, power, blessings, salvation, and exaltation. In that regard, God is no respecter of persons (see Acts 10:34; Doctrine and Covenants 38:16; Moroni 8:12; Doctrine and Covenants 1:35). As quoted partially in the Church's official statement, Nephi said:

"For he [the Lord] doeth that which is good among the children of men; and he doeth nothing save it be plain unto the children of men; and he inviteth them all to come unto him and partake of his goodness; and he denieth none that come unto him, black and white, bond and free, male and female; and he remembereth the heathen; and all are alike unto God, both Jew and Gentile" (2 Nephi 26:33).

Some criticize the Church today because women are not ordained to the priesthood and therefore do not "hold" the priesthood. How can this disparate treatment of men and women be reconciled? Again, we really do not have a complete understanding; however, women in the Church frequently exercise priesthood power and authority, though they are not ordained to priesthood offices.

Consider four ways in which this is so. First, through a setting apart by an authorized priesthood holder, women have priesthood authority to use in their callings in their wards and branches throughout the Church. They have all the authority they need to fulfill their callings and stewardships. What authority do they have? As Elder Dallin H. Oaks taught:

> We are not accustomed to speaking of women having the authority of the priesthood in their Church callings, but what other authority can it be? When a woman . . . is set apart to preach the gospel as a full-time missionary, she is given priesthood authority to perform a priesthood function. The same is true when a woman is set apart to function as an officer or teacher in a Church organization under the direction of one who holds the keys of the priesthood. Whoever functions in an office or calling received from one who holds priesthood keys exercises priesthood authority in performing her or his assigned duties.[10]

Second, women gain access to the power and blessings of God through receiving priesthood ordinances and making covenants.

Power comes from making and keeping baptismal covenants. Power comes from receiving the Holy Ghost. Power comes from making and keeping temple covenants. The power of godliness is thereby manifest in women's lives (see Doctrine and Covenants 84:20–21). As Elder Neil L. Andersen said, "The blessings of the priesthood are infinitely greater than the one who is asked to administer the gift."[11] LDS women who diligently make and keep covenants experience priesthood power in their lives.

Third, faithful women invite the blessings of heaven independent of priesthood ordination. The blessings of God's total priesthood power and authority are available to LDS women throughout the world. When miracles occur in a woman's life in the absence of conferred priesthood, she has complied with conditions to be blessed by God's total priesthood power and authority. Women tap into God's priesthood power and authority through faith and prayer. Women who pray and act in faith have regular access to God's priesthood power and authority. President Russell M. Nelson issued a plea to the women of the Church[12] to be the kind of women "who know how to make important things happen by their faith" and "who know how to call upon the powers of heaven." Women throughout the Church "speak with the power and authority of God" and demonstrate their faith by accepting and magnifying callings, serving missions, raising children, praying for guidance, and acting on the impressions from the Holy Ghost. Their faith gives them access to the powers of heaven to resist temptations, act in charity and goodness, build families, improve communities, and establish the Church.

This third way is complementary to, and not a substitute for, blessings received through conferred priesthood authority. It is not an "alternative" pathway to priesthood blessings to be used instead of those that are accessed through conferred priesthood.

Fourth, a woman participates in the fulness of the Melchizedek Priesthood through temple sealing to a worthy Melchizedek Priesthood holder. Exaltation and eternal life in the highest degree of the celestial kingdom are achieved only as the fulness of the priesthood is attained through building and achieving an eternal marriage. The highest intellectual and spiritual development of both men and women is to become as God is. Becoming as God cannot be achieved by men alone or women alone. Only through the sealing ordinances of the holy Melchizedek Priesthood, performed in the temple of the Lord and ratified by the Holy Spirit of Promise, and through faithful, righteous living can a man and a woman join in an eternal marriage unit wherein they may attain a fulness of the priesthood and exaltation together (see Doctrine and Covenants 132:18–19). All blessings, benefits, and inheritances of the Melchizedek Priesthood are equally shared and achieved by husband and wife if they keep their covenants and live in love, harmony, and cooperation in the Lord.

"Then shall they be gods, because they have no end; therefore shall they be from everlasting to everlasting, because they continue; then shall they be above all, because all things are subject unto them. Then shall they be gods, because they have all power, and the angels are subject unto them" (Doctrine and Covenants 132:19–20).

God offers to all His daughters multiple opportunities to have the fulness of His priesthood and to receive eternal power and blessings. This is where equality really matters. For some, the questions surrounding why God directs that only men are ordained to priesthood offices may be all consuming. They may feel that for God not to be a "respecter of persons" He must delegate tasks equally. However, participating in eternal equality before God is infinitely more important than being equally delegated earthly tasks.

Even with this understanding, some may still find the issue

of women and priesthood ordination troubling. But the time will come when those who remain faithful to the restored gospel of Jesus Christ despite their concerns will be blessed beyond measure. In the Lord's own time and in His own way, we will gain a clear understanding of His purposes. When that happens, we will all recognize that God has treated us with greater fairness, mercy, and compassion than we deserve or could have imagined.

The highest and greatest expression of priesthood power and authority is in the family. Families are integral to our loving Heavenly Father's plan; consequently, the interaction between priesthood and family is intertwined. Without the priesthood, the purpose of creation, the purpose of the earth itself, would come to naught. Without the restoration of the Melchizedek Priesthood and the sealing authority, "the whole earth would be utterly wasted" at the time of the Lord's Second Coming (Doctrine and Covenants 2:3). Without the priesthood and the welding link provided by the sealing authority, everyone would have "neither root nor branch," neither ancestry nor posterity (Malachi 4:1).

Heavenly Father's plan and His greatest desire is to have all of His children return to Him, saved from death and sin and exalted as families. "The Family: A Proclamation to the World" states: "The divine plan of happiness enables family relationships to be perpetuated beyond the grave. Sacred ordinances and covenants available in holy temples make it possible for individuals to return to the presence of God and for families to be united eternally."[13]

A correct understanding of God's plan helps us understand that both priesthood and family are necessary. In the ideal family, the husband and father presides in righteousness and uses the priesthood to bless the lives of his family members. Originally, priesthood was inherently patriarchal, and priesthood lineage was the same as a patriarchal lineage. God did not first create a church; He created a family. Later, God inspired prophets to organize a structure outside of the family, intended to support families. Then, priesthood outside of patriarchal lineage began.

For example, the seventy elders of Israel, spoken of in Exodus (24:1–11) and Numbers (11:16–25), appear to have performed a priesthood function that extended beyond their own families. The lesser judges to whom Moses delegated power performed priesthood functions beyond their own families (Exodus 18). Similarly, priesthood was used within a Church structure when Alma organized the Church of Christ at the Waters of Mormon (see Mosiah 18) and later organized units of that Church throughout the land of Zarahemla.

> And it came to pass that king Mosiah granted unto Alma that he might establish churches throughout all the land of Zarahemla; and gave him power to ordain priests and teachers over every church.
>
> Now this was done because there were so many people that they could not all be governed by one teacher; neither could they all hear the word of God in one assembly;
>
> Therefore they did assemble themselves together in different bodies, being called churches; every church having their priests and their teachers, and every priest preaching the word according as it was delivered to him by the mouth of Alma.
>
> And thus, notwithstanding there being many churches they were all one church, yea, even the church of God; for there was nothing preached in all the churches except it were repentance and faith in God.
>
> And now there were seven churches in the land of Zarahemla. And it came to pass that whosoever were desirous to take upon them the name of Christ, or of God, they did join the churches of God;
>
> And they were called the people of God. And the Lord

did pour out his Spirit upon them, and they were blessed, and prospered in the land. (Mosiah 25:19–24)

What is the role of the priesthood in the home when the priesthood exists without being tied to a patriarchal line? The priesthood holder should become a better husband and father as he incorporates the doctrine of the priesthood into his life. The principles that are necessary to use the priesthood are the same principles that will help a man be better at home.

A priesthood holder will learn that presiding in the home means that he serves in accordance with the doctrine of the priesthood. His life will be "founded on the teachings of the Lord Jesus Christ," and he will, with his wife as an equal partner, establish a home built on "principles of faith, prayer, repentance, forgiveness, respect, love, compassion, work, and wholesome recreational activity." He will seek to minister; he will acknowledge error and seek forgiveness; he will be quick to offer praise; he will be considerate of family members' preferences; he will feel the great weight of responsibility to provide "the necessities of life and protection" for his family; he will treat his wife with the utmost respect and deference. He will listen to understand the challenges facing each family member and then go about helping in the manner the Savior would. He will bless his family.[14]

NOTES

1. *Handbook 2: Administering the Church* (2010); section 2.0.

2. *Preach My Gospel* (2004), 44.

3. Brigham Young, in *Journal of Discourses,* 26 vols. (1854–86), 15:137. Other statements by Brigham Young in this reference include:
   "And when our spirits receive our bodies, and through our faithfulness we are worthy to be crowned, we will then receive authority to produce both spirit and body. But these keys we cannot receive in the flesh.
   "We have not the power in the flesh to create and bring forth or produce a spirit [with all the vaunted knowledge of the experts in the world, this has not been given to man]; but we have the power to produce [with the help of

God] a temporal body [for our children]. The germ of this, God has placed within us. . . . Herein, brethren, you can perceive that we have not finished, and cannot finish our work, while we live here [on the earth], no more than Jesus did while he was in the flesh.

". . . fashion kingdoms [or] organize matter, for [that is] beyond our capacity and calling, beyond this world. In the resurrection, men who have been faithful and diligent in all things in the flesh, [who] have kept their first and second estate, and [are] worthy to be crowned Gods, even the sons of God, will be ordained to organize matter. How much matter do you suppose there is between here and some of the fixed stars which we can see? Enough to frame many, very many millions of such earths as this, yet it is now so diffused, clear and pure, that we look through it and behold the stars. Yet the matter is there. Can you form any conception of this? Can you form any idea of the minuteness of matter?"

4. Spencer W. Kimball, "Our Great Potential," *Ensign,* May 1977.

5. See Terryl Givens and Fiona Givens, *The Crucible of Doubt: Reflections on the Quest for Faith* (2014), 87.

6. Man, however, cannot take such priesthood power unto himself; it must be conferred by God through His servants (see Hebrews 5:4; Doctrine and Covenants 1:38). Unauthorized use of the priesthood is invalid, sinful, and frequently punished (see the examples of Korah [Numbers 16], Miriam [Exodus 15:20; Numbers 12], Uzza [1 Chronicles 13:10], Saul [1 Samuel 13:5–14], Uzziah [2 Chronicles 26], and Sceva's sons [Acts 19:13–17]).

7. *Teachings of Presidents of the Church: Joseph Smith* (2007), 108–9.

8. Official statement released by the Church on February 29, 2012, titled "The Church and Race: 'All Are Alike Unto God.'" *Church News,* March 3, 2012, 5; accessed at http://www.mormonnewsroom.org/article/race-church. See also www.lds.org/topics/race-and-the-priesthood?lang=eng.

9. Ibid.

10. Dallin H. Oaks, "The Keys and Authority of the Priesthood," *Ensign,* May 2014.

11. Neil L. Andersen, "Power in the Priesthood," *Ensign,* November 2013.

12. Russell M. Nelson, "A Plea to My Sisters," *Ensign,* November 2015.

13. "The Family: A Proclamation to the World," *Ensign,* November 2010.

14. Ibid.

Chapter 2

PRIESTHOOD OFFICES AND KEYS

And by the keys which I have given shall they be led.
—DOCTRINE AND COVENANTS 35:25

In the Church, priesthood offices and keys have nothing to do with rooms and locks. Their meanings are metaphorical. Individuals who receive the Aaronic or Melchizedek Priesthood are each ordained to an office in that priesthood. The term *office* refers to a position of priesthood authority. The offices of deacon, teacher, priest, and bishop are Aaronic Priesthood positions. The offices of elder, high priest, patriarch, Seventy, and Apostle are Melchizedek Priesthood positions. Bishops, however, hold the office of high priest in the Melchizedek Priesthood although their office is in the Aaronic Priesthood (see Doctrine and Covenants 107:15–17).

In the Melchizedek Priesthood, the offices of elder, high priest, and patriarch are generally found in a stake. Those so ordained are "standing" ministers," meaning that they are not assigned to travel away from their communities as part of their calling (Doctrine and Covenants 124:137; 84:111).

In contrast, those ordained to the offices of Seventy and Apostle are special witnesses of the name of the Savior in all the world, "thus differing from other officers in the church in the duties of their calling" (Doctrine and Covenants 107:23, 25; 124:139). They travel away from their communities as part of their calling.

The term *priesthood keys* is used in two different ways. The first refers to a specific right or privilege conferred upon all who receive the Aaronic or Melchizedek Priesthood. In other words, everyone upon whom the priesthood is conferred receives some priesthood keys. For instance, Aaronic Priesthood holders receive the keys of the ministering of angels and the keys of the preparatory gospel of repentance and of baptism by immersion for the remission of sins (see Doctrine and Covenants 13:1; 84:26–27). Melchizedek Priesthood holders receive the key of the mysteries of the kingdom, the key of the knowledge of God, and the keys of all the spiritual blessings of the Church (see Doctrine and Covenants 84:19; 107:18). Holders of both the Aaronic and Melchizedek Priesthoods have the right to exercise authority and power in the name of Jesus Christ, but with limits.

The second way the term *priesthood keys* is used refers to leadership. Priesthood leaders receive additional priesthood keys, the right to preside over an organizational division of the Church or a quorum. In this regard, priesthood keys are the authority and power to direct, lead, and govern in the Church. Other priesthood holders administer saving ordinances and serve in the priesthood within the limits outlined by those who hold the priesthood keys. Leaders receive priesthood keys from those in authority over them.

It is easy to see why keys of priesthood leadership are necessary. Consider what would happen if everyone who has earned the right to play on a basketball team chose to do whatever he wanted to do whenever he wanted to do it on the court. If you are on such a team, you will never win. Someone must be designated to bring order and structure to the play. That individual could be a player-coach. He is responsible for training others, running practices, encouraging and critiquing, and dividing up responsibilities. Without such order, many would shoot every time they had the ball. Few would play defense. The player-coach ensures that the individual players play as a coordinated team. Priesthood leaders perform a similar function. They are given keys of presidency to lead, teach, organize, and encourage those over whom they preside.

When a person holding priesthood keys is released, he no longer holds those priesthood keys. One reason priesthood keys are given is to maintain order and ensure that the Church operates correctly. Priesthood keys are given by the laying on of hands when the priesthood holder is set apart to the leadership position. Among local priesthood holders, only stake presidents, mission presidents, temple presidents, bishops, branch presidents, and quorum presidents hold keys pertaining to their respective offices. It is important to remember that a man does not receive additional priesthood when he is given priesthood keys of leadership. Priesthood keys provide order and predictability in the Church. This creates the perfect team to assist the Lord in His work.

Chapter 3

PRIESTHOOD KEYS AND THE HOLY APOSTLESHIP

The Twelve Apostles . . . officiate . . . under the direction
of the Presidency of the Church . . . holding the keys.
—DOCTRINE AND COVENANTS 107:23, 33, 35

On Thursday, October 8, 2015, on the fourth floor of the Salt Lake Temple, in my first meeting of the Council of the First Presidency and Quorum of the Twelve, all fourteen living Apostles placed their hands on my head and, with President Thomas S. Monson acting as voice, I was ordained an Apostle of the Lord Jesus Christ. Sister Renlund was present for the experience, which for us was Pentecostal.

Part of the ordination included this statement: "We give you every right, gift, authority, and the keys of this sacred office, including the keys of prophet, seer, and revelator to be shared with your Brethren in this circle."[1] I have since pondered what it means to share the keys of prophet, seer, and revelator with the other living Apostles. It is an important point in Church governance—important for me as a new member of the Twelve, and equally important for all members of the Church. Understanding this phrase, "the keys of prophet, seer, and revelator to be shared with your Brethren," is foundational to understanding how the doctrine of the Church is established, how we can know God's will in the Church, and who has a right to declare new doctrine and officially proclaim God's will to the Saints.

The idea of "shared apostolic keys" could have several meanings. First, it could mean that there is just one set of keys that is passed around. This is suggested in Bertel Thorvaldsen's masterpiece sculptures of the Christus and the Twelve Apostles in *Vor Frue Kirke* (the Church of Our Lady) in Copenhagen, Denmark; it is only Peter who is portrayed holding keys. Second, it could mean that each new Apostle is given a set of keys that he can exercise in any way he wants. In this situation, the keys would be considered "shared" because all hold the same keys. Third, it could mean that each Apostle has a set of keys but that they are used and exercised only in harmony with the others and under the direction of the President of the Church. In this third meaning, limits or constraints are placed on the exercise of the keys an Apostle has been given.

The historical record of the Restoration answers the question of how apostolic keys are shared. Many aspects of the Restoration took a long time to unfold; it was and is a process, not an event. We can liken it to a large, 10,000-piece jigsaw puzzle. Over time, the Lord directs the placement of the puzzle pieces, until the whole picture is clear. But which puzzle piece is needed at any given time becomes evident only as the outline for its need is known. The scriptures refer to this process as learning line upon line and precept upon precept (see Isaiah 28:10, 13; 2 Nephi 28:30; Doctrine and Covenants 98:12; 128:21).

One of the first questions that arose after the Church was organized was, "Who can receive revelation for the Church?" An early convert, Hiram Page, professed to be receiving revelations concerning the building of Zion and the order of the Church. Several members, including Oliver Cowdery, were deceived by his declarations. In September 1830, Joseph Smith received a revelation directed to Oliver Cowdery. In this revelation, the Lord stated that "no one shall be appointed to receive commandments and revelations in this church excepting my servant Joseph Smith, Jun." The revelation also made it clear that Hiram Page's revelations were "not of [God] and that Satan deceiveth him" (Doctrine and Covenants 28:2, 11; see also section heading).

This revelation clarified who was authorized to receive revelation for the Church. At that time, it was Joseph Smith Jr., the Church's first elder. He alone was God's spokesman.

As the Restoration continued, Joseph Smith received direction to organize not only a First Presidency but also a Quorum of Twelve Apostles. In addition to the functional assignment of being a traveling high council in preaching the gospel, the Twelve were given priesthood keys. At the time of the organization of the Quorum of the Twelve Apostles in February 1835, each of the Apostles received the keys of the kingdom—all the keys that Joseph had received up to that point. It is also clear that the same keys were held by each member of the Twelve.[2] Therefore, this refutes the notion that there is just one set of apostolic keys that is passed around.

Additional keys were given to Joseph Smith after 1835, including those received by Joseph Smith and Oliver Cowdery in the Kirtland Temple on April 3, 1836 (see Doctrine and Covenants 110:11–16 and section heading). These additional keys were also conferred on the Twelve Apostles. Wilford Woodruff reported a meeting of the Apostles with Joseph Smith in March 1844. Elder Woodruff stated:

I remember the last speech that [Joseph Smith] ever gave us before his death. . . . [Joseph] said: "I have had sealed upon my head every key, every power, every principle of life and salvation that God has ever given to any man who ever lived upon the face of the earth . . . Now," said he, addressing the Twelve, "I have sealed upon your heads every key, every power, and every principle which the Lord has sealed upon my head. . . . I tell you, the burden of this kingdom now rests upon your shoulders; you have got to bear it off in all the world, and if you don't do it you will be damned."[3]

The Woodruff account is corroborated by Parley P. Pratt. He wrote:

[Joseph Smith] was led, before his death, to call the Twelve together, from time to time, and to instruct them in all things pertaining to the kingdom, ordinances, and government of God. He often observed that he was laying the foundation, but it would remain for the Twelve to complete the building. Said he, "I know not why; but for some reason I am constrained to . . . confer upon the Twelve all the ordinances, keys, covenants, endowments, and sealing ordinances of the priesthood. . . . The kingdom of God will roll on, as I have now finished the work which was laid upon me."[4]

During Joseph Smith's lifetime, he alone was God's spokesman. But, under the direction of heaven, he prepared the Church for his absence by conferring all the keys and authorities that he had received on each member of the Twelve. He did not confer the keys on any one member but on each one of them. Every member of the Quorum of the Twelve held all the keys of the kingdom of God and had the priesthood authority necessary to hold every position in the Church.[5]

Because each Apostle held equivalent keys, confusion arose about who could speak for the Church and who could declare doctrine that would be binding on Church members. Could each exercise his keys any way he wanted? This question was the subject of a meeting of the First Presidency and Quorum of the Twelve before April conference in 1860. Two days were spent discussing to what extent individual members of the First Presidency and the Twelve were free to express their own views on certain doctrines in their public discourses.

At one point, Orson Hyde verbalized ambivalent feelings as he said: "When the Prophet pronounces upon (revealed) doctrines, it is for us to repudiate ours, and sustain his. . . . As to whether we should sustain the Prophet in every scientifical subject, contrary to our own judgment, it might not be policy to say that, as (it) involves a principle of absolutism which would not look well."[6]

After two days of deliberation, the Apostles came to an agreement. They said that they would "keep as far away from the precipice" as possible by avoiding the public discussion of debatable subjects "that could put one in a rough place." They also signed the following statement: "No member of the Church has the right to publish any doctrines as the doctrines of the Church . . . without first submitting them for examination and approval to the First Presidency and the Twelve."[7]

While this statement clearly resolved the issue regarding members other than the Council of the First Presidency and Quorum of the Twelve, the deliberation did not fully resolve the question as to whether individuals who had been ordained as prophets, seers, and revelators needed to follow the same process as other members. Could they authoritatively and independently promulgate doctrine to and for the Church? The answer is definitively spelled out in the third official proclamation from the First Presidency and Quorum of the Twelve, issued in 1865. This proclamation is a thorough re-buke of Orson Pratt, who was one of the original Apostles in this dispensation, ordained in 1835.

Orson Pratt had written several articles over the years that the First Presidency and Twelve found objectionable. The proclamation cites many of these teachings at length. A representative writing by Orson Pratt is this one:

> Each part of [the God-like] substance is all-wise and all-powerful . . . when we worship the Spirit, we do not merely worship a personal substance or a widely diffused substance, but we worship the attributes and qualities of this substance . . . a living, self-moving fluid substance . . . each particle of this Holy Spirit knows, every instant, how to act upon the other materials of nature with which it is immediately associ-ated: it knows how to vary the gravitating tendency of a par-ticle of matter, every moment, precisely in the inverse ratio of the square of its distance from every other particle in the universe.[8]

The First Presidency and the Twelve took issue. They said:

> We have quoted some of the items . . . which strike us as being most objectionable. They are self-confounding and conflict one with another. . . . There are great and important truths connected with the eternities of our God and with man's existence past, present and future, which the Almighty, in his wisdom, sees fit to conceal from the children of men. [The ideas that Orson Pratt had espoused] are mere hypoth-eses, and should be perused and accepted as such, and not as doctrines of the Church. . . . No member of the Church has the right to publish any doctrines, as the doctrines of the Church of Jesus Christ of Latter-day Saints, without first

submitting them for examination and approval [by] the First Presidency and the Twelve.

This statement makes it clear that even members of the First Presidency and Quorum of the Twelve must first submit proposed doctrinal opinions to the First Presidency and the Twelve for approval before promulgating them as official.

The proclamation continues:

> There is but one man upon the earth, at one time, who holds the keys to receive commandments and revelations for the Church, and who has the authority to write doctrines by way of commandment unto the Church. And any man who so far forgets the order instituted by the Lord as to write and publish what may be termed new doctrines, without consulting with the First Presidency of the Church respecting them, places himself in a false position, and exposes himself to the power of darkness by violating his Priesthood . . . [and] will be liable to lose his Priesthood.[9]

The crux of the proclamation is this statement: "There is but one man upon the earth, at one time, who holds the keys to receive commandments and revelations for the Church, and who has the authority to write doctrines by way of commandment unto the Church." It informed Orson Pratt, as well as the world, that he was out of bounds. He had no right to stand as a prophet, seer, and revelator and espouse his own thinking without sanction by the Council of the First Presidency and the Twelve.

Orson Pratt must have been embarrassed. But he was also sufficiently humble to issue the following statement: "I, therefore, embrace the present opportunity of publicly expressing my most sincere regret that I have ever published the least thing which meets with the disapprobation of the highest authorities of the Church."[10]

Poor Orson Pratt was the test case not only for all future Apostles but for the whole Church. His experience taught every member, including the Apostles, that an Apostle can only speak authoritatively for the Church under the direction of and with the sanction of the First Presidency and the Twelve.

I know, better than anyone else, that not every thought I have is inspired of heaven. I still need to work to clarify revelation and inspiration. But if I were to inform Sister Renlund that the Holy Ghost works through the intermediary of the Higgs boson subatomic particle and that it in turn interacts with spiritual matter with a force that is inversely proportional to the square of the distance from the spiritual fluid, she (and everyone else) should know that such ideas can be discounted as opinion and not as revelation.

We will always be on the right path when we follow those we sustain as prophets, seers, and revelators. I have observed that members of the Twelve frequently confer with their quorum members to ensure that their individual directions are in harmony with the quorum. It is now well established that members of the Quorum of the Twelve do not individually pronounce doctrine that is not in harmony with their Brethren. In other words, there are limits or constraints placed on the exercise of the keys an Apostle has been given. These constraints involve the primacy of the senior Apostle and the requirement of unanimity.

Just like Joseph Smith, the senior Apostle, the President of the Church, is the only one on earth authorized to exercise all priesthood keys. President Russell M. Nelson notes: "When a President of the Church dies, the First Presidency is dissolved and the counselors take their places in the Quorum of the Twelve Apostles. The Quorum of the Twelve then presides over the Church until the First Presidency is reorganized. That period of time is known as an apostolic interregnum. Historically, that interval has varied in length from four days to three and a half years."[11]

Beginning with the administration of Lorenzo Snow in 1898, Presidents of the Church have been formally set apart or ordained by the other living prophets, seers, and revelators. Before this time, it was not felt to be necessary since the senior Apostle already held all the keys necessary to lead the Church as its President.

George Q. Cannon recorded the change in policy as follows:

> President [Lorenzo] Snow had expressed a desire to be ordained (to use his own words) as President of the Church. I related to the brethren [that when] . . . I had been selected as one of [Brigham Young's] counselors . . . I had asked him whether it was necessary to be set apart for that position. His reply to me was that he had not set apart . . . any of his counselors, for the reason that they held their position by virtue of their Apostleship. The feeling, however, today [1898] was that it would be a very appropriate thing for Brother Snow to be ordained, and a vote was taken to the effect that it should be done.
>
> We all laid our hands upon him, and at his request I pronounced the blessing upon him and set him apart to preside over the Church of Jesus Christ of Latter-day Saints. I was then set apart to be his First Counselor, and President Joseph F. Smith was set apart to be his Second Counselor.[12]

Elder Franklin D. Richards recorded that all ordained Apostles placed their hands on President Snow's head as he was set apart and blessed.[13]

Since 1898, every Church President has been set apart under the hands of his fellow Apostles. In 1951, when David O. McKay became Church President, the term *ordain* began to be used instead of or in addition to the term *set apart*.[14] This practice has continued to the present day.[15] It is not only a comfort and blessing to the President of the Church, it is also a formal submission by each of the Apostles to the Presidency of the senior Apostle, submitting their individually held keys to his authority and position. This action "ordains" one Apostle to be the only one on earth authorized to exercise all priesthood keys. The principle involved has been emphasized by many over the years.

President Gordon B. Hinckley said: "Only the President of the Church has the right to exercise [the keys] in their fulness. He may delegate the exercise of various of them to one or more of his Brethren. Each has the keys but is authorized to use them only to the degree granted him by the prophet of the Lord."[16] This protects all members of the Church because they know who can pronounce doctrine for the entire Church.

The other protection that the Lord has provided is the requirement of unanimity in the presiding councils of the Church.[17] In 1938, Elder Stephen L Richards taught this principle. He said:

> In formulating their interpretations and decisions they [the First Presidency] always confer with the Council of the Twelve Apostles who by revelation are appointed to assist and act with them in the government of the Church. When, therefore, a judgment is reached and proclaimed by these officers it becomes binding upon all members of the Church, individual views to the contrary notwithstanding.[18]

Elder James E. Faust further explained: "This requirement of unanimity provides a check on bias and personal idiosyncrasies. It ensures that God rules through the Spirit, not man through majority or compromise. It ensures that the best wisdom and experience is focused on an issue before the deep, unassailable impressions of revealed direction are received. It guards against the foibles of man."[19] In understanding the will of the Lord, both the primacy of the senior Apostle and the requirement for unanimity are recognized as protections for the Church.

Some have taught that the keys, authority, and power given to each member of the Twelve lie dormant[20] "until he becomes [the] senior apostle and is [then] in a position of presidency to direct the labors and the work of all others."[21] However, in isolation or without a full understanding, this may lead some to a false notion that the conferral of authority and keys on each Apostle is simply God's backup plan and that those keys, and those Apostles, are of little utility until some future day. On the contrary, each Apostle exercises the keys he has been given to the full extent possible, in harmony with his fellow Apostles, and as constrained by the direction of the President of the Church.

Understanding the role of the senior Apostle and the requirement of unanimity among all prophets, seers, and revelators, members may know God's will for His Church in the following ways:

First, when God's will is declared by the prophet and sustained by the Council of the First Presidency and the Twelve, it can be considered doctrine. In the past, we have seen two official declarations, one regarding polygamy and the other about the priesthood. The Church has accepted Doctrine and Covenants 138 as doctrine in a similar manner.[22] More commonly, we see God's will conveyed in a letter from the First Presidency.

Second, when all the prophets, seers, and revelators, acting as one, make doctrinal pronouncements, they can be considered official. "The Family: A Proclamation to the World"[23] and "The Living Christ"[24] are examples of this.

Finally, in this modern era, general conference addresses by members of the First Presidency and Quorum of the Twelve expound, clarify, and emphasize established doctrines. The messages are scrutinized, reviewed, and approved by the First Presidency and members of the Twelve before being given. Given the extent to which these messages are prepared and delivered in compliance with the following criterion, they merit special attention: "And whatsoever they shall speak when moved upon by the Holy Ghost shall be scripture, shall be the will of the Lord, shall be the mind of the Lord, shall be the word of the Lord, shall be the voice of the Lord, and the power of God unto salvation" (Doctrine and Covenants 68:40).

For this reason, President Ezra Taft Benson taught at the conclusion of the April 1988 general conference, "For the next six months, your conference edition of the *Ensign* should stand next to your standard works and be referred to frequently."[25]

As an ordained Apostle, holding the keys of prophet, seer, and revelator to be shared with the others who are similarly ordained, I am grateful for the clarifications and constraints that have been revealed over the decades. These provide the protections God intended in this, the only true and living Church on the face of the earth (see Doctrine and Covenants 1:30). In the Lord's living Church, the standard is very high. God's will is not revealed to just one individual. It must be revealed to all fifteen prophets, seers, and revelators. All so ordained must labor to receive the revelation and achieve the unity God requires. Additionally, all Church members can, if they will, receive confirmatory revelation of the will of God as it has been revealed through His servants.

NOTES

1. Ordination of Dale G. Renlund, October 8, 2015, by President Thomas S. Monson. Personal record.

2. Minute Book 1 (Kirtland Council Minute Book), February 14, 1835, Church History Library. Orson Hyde and William Smith were both told in their ordinations that they were "equal with [their] brethren in holding the keys of the kingdom."

3. Wilford Woodruff, in *Teachings of Presidents of the Church: Joseph Smith* (2007), 532.

4. Parley P. Pratt, "Proclamation to The Church of Jesus Christ of Latter-day Saints," January 1, 1845, in *Millennial Star,* 5, no. 10 (March 1845): 151.

5. See Harold B. Lee, in Conference Report, April 1970, 123.

6. Orson Hyde, in Leonard J. Arrington, *Brigham Young: American Moses* (1986), 304–5.

7. In ibid.

8. "Proclamation of the Twelve," as published in *Millennial Star,* 27, no. 42 (October 21, 1865): 661.

9. Ibid., 662–63.

10. Orson Pratt, "To the Saints in All the World," *Millennial Star,* 27, no. 44 (November 4, 1865): 698.

11. Russell M. Nelson, "Sustaining the Prophets," *Ensign,* November 2014, n. 15.

12. George Q. Cannon journal, October 10, 1898, Church History Library.

13. See Franklin D. Richards journal, October 10, 1898, Church History Library.

14. "President Kimball then took his seat in the middle of the room, and as all those present placed their hands upon his head . . . then, with President Benson being mouth, in a beautiful prayer and blessing, Spencer Woolley Kimball was ordained and set apart as prophet, seer, and revelator and president of The Church of Jesus Christ of Latter-day Saints" (N. Eldon Tanner, "Chosen of the Lord," *Ensign,* May 1974). "But authority to exercise those keys is restricted to the President of the Church. At his passing, that authority becomes operative in the senior Apostle, who is then named, set apart, and ordained a prophet and President by his associates of the Council of the Twelve" (Gordon B. Hinckley, "Come and Partake," *Ensign,* May 1986). "Then more recently, the day after his funeral, in July 1972, there came to the Presidency of the Church . . . newly ordained and set apart prophet and President, Harold B. Lee" (Spencer W. Kimball, *The Teachings of Spencer W. Kimball* [1982], 467). "President George Albert Smith, President of the Church of Jesus Christ of Latter-day Saints, the Presiding High Priest of the Church, the prophet, seer and revelator, ordained and set apart thereto by those having authority will now close this conference with his final instruction" (J. Reuben Clark Jr., in Conference Report, April 1950, 167).

15. Interestingly, Doctrine and Covenants 107:22, when speaking of the First Presidency, uses the word *ordain.* At the time, *ordain* and *set apart* were often used interchangeably. Nonetheless, the passage reads: "Of the Melchizedek Priesthood, three Presiding High Priests, chosen by the body, appointed and

ordained to that office, and upheld by the confidence, faith, and prayer of the church, form a quorum of the Presidency of the Church."

16. Gordon B. Hinckley, "The Church Is on Course," *Ensign,* November 1992.

17. Doctrine and Covenants 107:27–29 states, "And every decision made by either of these quorums must be by the unanimous voice of the same; that is, every member in each quorum must be agreed to its decisions, in order to make their decisions of the same power or validity one with the other— A majority may form a quorum when circumstances render it impossible to be otherwise—Unless this is the case, their decisions are not entitled to the same blessings which the decisions of a quorum of three presidents were anciently, who were ordained after the order of Melchizedek, and were righteous and holy men."

18. Stephen L Richards, in Conference Report, October 1938, 116.

19. James E. Faust, "Continuous Revelation," *Ensign,* November 1989.

20. Joseph Fielding Smith, *Doctrines of Salvation,* 3 vols. (1954–56), 3:157.

21. Bruce R. McConkie, "Succession in the Presidency," January 8, 1974, *BYU Speeches of the Year.*

22. See Doctrine and Covenants, Official Declaration 1, Official Declaration 2, and section 138. Doctrine and Covenants 137 and Doctrine and Covenants 138 were approved to be added to the Pearl of Great Price by the Council of the First Presidency and Quorum of the Twelve in March 1976. The revelations were presented at the April 1976 general conference to the Church and were sustained as part of the standard works of the Church.

23. "The Family: A Proclamation to the World," *Ensign,* November 2010.

24. "The Living Christ: The Testimony of the Apostles, The Church of Jesus Christ of Latter-day Saints," *Ensign,* April 2000.

25. Ezra Taft Benson, "Come Unto Christ, and Be Perfected in Him," *Ensign,* May 1988. The talk was read by President Gordon B. Hinckley due to President Benson's poor health.

Chapter 4

THE PRIESTHOOD
BLESSES THE
PRIESTHOOD HOLDER

The covenant . . . is confirmed upon you for your sakes.

—DOCTRINE AND COVENANTS 84:48

The Lord has declared that the priesthood exists for two primary reasons: to bless the individual who holds it and to fulfill the work of salvation through the priesthood holder's exercise of it. In September 1832, elders began returning from their missions in the Eastern States and reporting their labors. The Prophet Joseph Smith received a revelation on the priesthood in which the Savior taught about the covenant associated with the Melchizedek Priesthood and these two primary reasons for the priesthood:

"And the Father teacheth him [the one holding the Melchizedek Priesthood] of the covenant which he [Heavenly Father] has renewed and confirmed upon you, which is confirmed upon you *for your sakes,* and not for your sakes only, but *for the sake of the whole world*" (Doctrine and Covenants 84:48; emphasis added).

Through revelation we understand that the priesthood blesses the priesthood holder and he holds the priesthood to bless the world through its use. This chapter considers how the priesthood blesses the individual priesthood holder.

Abraham recognized that the priesthood blesses the life of the priesthood holder and, by extension, his family. He actively sought these blessings.

> And, finding there was greater *happiness* and *peace and rest* for me, I sought for the blessings of the fathers, and the right whereunto I should be ordained to administer the same; having been myself a follower of righteousness, desiring also to be one who possessed great knowledge, and to be a greater follower of righteousness, and to possess a greater *knowledge,* and to be a *father of many nations,* a *prince of peace,* and desiring to receive instructions, and to keep the commandments of God, I became a *rightful heir,* a High Priest, holding the right belonging to the fathers. (Abraham 1:2; emphasis added)

Abraham identified the blessings of holding the Melchizedek Priesthood as: greater happiness, peace and rest, righteousness, knowledge, and family blessings. He recognized that receiving the priesthood would result in his becoming a prince of peace and a rightful heir to God. These blessings are the greatest the Lord can promise and are also offered to priesthood holders today. Let's consider each blessing individually.

Greater happiness. Great joy comes to individuals as they accept the gospel and make covenants for themselves. Greater happiness comes to a priesthood holder as he aligns his purpose with the work and glory of God, "to bring to pass the immortality and eternal life of man" (Moses 1:39; Doctrine and Covenants 18:15–16). Because he holds the priesthood, a priesthood holder can officiate in priesthood ordinances. As he helps others to make and keep the covenants associated with each ordinance along the path to exaltation, he progresses steadily toward being like God. The Spirit is with him, prompting and directing his life.

Greater peace and rest. As a priesthood holder progresses along the path toward being like God, he can know that he stands approved before Him. This peace and rest can be contrasted with the anxiety that exists when one is unsure of one's standing before God. Peace of mind leads to restful existence even during turbulent times.

A life filled with priesthood service qualifies for the peace of the "Comforter," the Holy Ghost. Worthy priesthood holders qualify to attend the temple and receive a fulness of the Holy Ghost and, by extension, a fulness of comfort and peace (Doctrine and Covenants 109:15). To those endowed in temples (both men and women), these additional promises of peace are made:

> That thy servants may go forth from this house armed with thy power, and that thy name may be upon them, and thy glory be round about them, and thine angels have charge over them. . . .
>
> That no weapon formed against them shall prosper; that he who diggeth a pit for them shall fall into the same himself;
>
> That no combination of wickedness shall have power to rise up and prevail. (Doctrine and Covenants 109:22, 25–26)

An endowed priesthood holder experiences this kind of peace and rest.

Greater righteousness. As a priesthood holder performs priesthood functions, he is refined. The principles that govern the use of the priesthood distill on his soul as dews from heaven. His natural-man tendencies are replaced with Christlike attributes. Impurities are eliminated just as in a refiner's fire.

An analogy can be drawn from the physical sciences. In the solid state, the purity of an element can be assessed by its melting point. The greater the impurities, the lower the melting point. Conversely, the greater the purity of the element, the greater the temperature must be before the element changes from solid to liquid. The melting point of pure gold is 1,948 degrees Fahrenheit (1,064 degrees Celsius). Any impurity will decrease the melting temperature. Gold that is 90 percent pure will melt at approximately 1,938 degrees Fahrenheit (1,059 degrees Celsius). Pure gold tolerates more heat than impure gold does.

The same is true for a priesthood holder. He becomes refined through his righteousness. The purer he becomes, the more he can do, the more he can withstand. He becomes more trustworthy, more capable, and more dependable.

Greater knowledge. The promise of greater knowledge is repeatedly given by God to those who seek and serve Him. For instance, He has said: "That which is of God is light; and he that receiveth light, and continueth in God, receiveth more light; and that light groweth brighter and brighter until the perfect day" (Doctrine and Covenants 50:24).

Being on the covenant path leads to greater and greater light. Light is spiritual knowledge. Abraham knew that if he embarked on the path of righteousness, embodied by those who accepted the priesthood, his quest for spiritual and temporal knowledge would be rewarded. In general, though, this knowledge is the kind that enables one to serve better. This is made clear in a commandment the Lord gave to priesthood holders in the beginning of this dispensation:

> And I give unto you a commandment that you shall teach one another the doctrine of the kingdom.
>
> Teach ye diligently and my grace shall attend you, that you may be instructed more perfectly in theory, in principle, in doctrine, in the law of the gospel, in all things that pertain

unto the kingdom of God, that are expedient for you to understand;

Of things both in heaven and in the earth, and under the earth; things which have been, things which are, things which must shortly come to pass; things which are at home, things which are abroad; the wars and the perplexities of the nations, and the judgments which are on the land; and a knowledge also of countries and of kingdoms—

That ye may be prepared in all things when I shall send you again to magnify the calling whereunto I have called you, and the mission with which I have commissioned you. (Doctrine and Covenants 88:77–80)

Spiritual knowledge is not granted to satisfy idle curiosity but to fulfill God's purposes in His work.

After being converted by the teaching of Abinadi, Alma the Elder established a church. Baptism was performed, and priests were ordained to teach the people. These priests "were not to depend upon the people for their support; but for their labor they were to receive the grace of God, that they might wax strong in the Spirit, having the knowledge of God, that they might teach with power and authority from God" (Mosiah 18:26). For their labor, they received the grace of God, a greater portion of the Spirit, and greater knowledge. The express purpose for this "wage" is to teach with greater power and authority.

Family blessings. Abraham sought to be a father of many nations with a large posterity. He may have understood that he would receive eternal increase. The Lord accomplishes this by sealing His children to both forebears and posterity in holy temples.

On one occasion, through the prophet Malachi, the Lord expressed some sadness over Israel's complaint that He had somehow not held up His end of the covenant.

Your words have been stout against me, saith the Lord. Yet ye say, What have we spoken so much against thee?

Ye have said, It is vain to serve God: and what profit is it that we have kept his ordinance, and that we have walked mournfully before the Lord of hosts?

And now we call the proud happy; yea, they that work wickedness are set up; yea, they that tempt God are even delivered.

Then they that feared the Lord spake often one to another: and the Lord hearkened, and heard it, and a book of remembrance was written before him for them that feared the Lord, and that thought upon his name.

And they shall be mine, saith the Lord of hosts, in that day when I make up my jewels; and I will spare them, as a man spareth his own son that serveth him.

Then shall ye return, and discern between the righteous and the wicked, between him that serveth God and him that serveth him not.

For, behold, the day cometh, that shall burn as an oven; and all the proud, yea, and all that do wickedly, shall be stubble: and the day that cometh shall burn them up, saith the Lord of hosts, that it shall leave them neither root nor branch.

But unto you that fear my name shall the Sun of righteousness arise with healing in his wings; and ye shall go forth, and grow up as calves of the stall. (Malachi 3:13–18; 4:1–2)

The time will come when the difference between the righteous and the wicked will be clear. The righteous will be sealed, by priesthood authority, to both their roots (their forebears) and their branches (their posterity). Whatever unfairness has occurred will be resolved. Whatever wounds have been incurred will be healed. The vagaries of an unpredictable environment will be removed and the ultimate protection will be offered, resulting in great joy. In that day, the Lord says, we will be able to judge between those who have followed His commands and those who have not.

Prince of peace. Abraham desired to become a prince of peace like Melchizedek, who was known to his people as the Prince of peace.

"And now, Melchizedek was a priest of this order [the Holy Priesthood, after the Order of the Son of God]; wherefore he obtained peace in Salem, and was called the Prince of peace. And this Melchizedek, having thus established righteousness, was called the king of heaven by his people, or, in other words, the King of peace" (JST, Genesis 14:33, 36; Doctrine and Covenants 107:3).

The peace that is spoken of is not just a freedom from conflict but a reconciliation to God through the Atonement of Jesus Christ.

Being a prince of peace naturally involves being a peacemaker or promoting peace (see Matthew 5:9; 3 Nephi 12:9). The scriptures also refer to a peacemaker as one who proclaims the gospel (see Mosiah 15:11–18). By preaching the gospel, the preacher invites people to come unto Jesus Christ so that they may be reconciled with Heavenly Father.

Rightful heir. Abraham also desired to be a rightful heir to the blessings promised to the fathers. In other words, Abraham desired to be a joint-heir with Jesus Christ, who, as the perfectly obedient firstborn, inherits all that Heavenly Father has. All of God's sons and daughters who have been born again through the Atonement of Christ become joint-heirs, rightful heirs to the inheritance (see John 1:12; Romans 8:14, 16–17; Mosiah 27:25; 3 Nephi 9:17; Doctrine and Covenants 11:30; 25:1; Moses 6:68; 7:1). Using God's incomparable mathematics and the Savior's generosity, the addition of shareholders does not diminish the share each receives. All receive all that Heavenly Father has.

The blessings Abraham sought are also promised today to each priesthood holder. For his sake, for his family, for his happiness, for his peace, for his righteousness, for his knowledge, for his reconciliation, and for his inheritance, the priesthood holder can participate in God's priesthood. But with this great gift comes his obligation to bless others. For the priesthood is not for his sake alone.

Chapter 5

THE PRIESTHOOD
BLESSES OTHERS

. . . preach . . . bind up . . . proclaim . . . comfort . . .
—ISAIAH 61:1–3

Although a priesthood holder is blessed by holding the priesthood, a primary purpose of the priesthood is to bless others. In fact, the blessings the individual priesthood holder is promised are conditioned on his serving others. One of the ways a priesthood holder serves others is through a priesthood quorum. A quorum is defined as a class, a fraternity, and a service unit.[1] And it is through his quorum that a priesthood holder's service is often organized and given.

The priesthood is not the only organization that can provide fraternity. Other organizations do so in an exemplary manner. Some organizations provide the opportunity for continuing education. The priesthood is not necessary for classroom experiences and the acquisition of new and exciting knowledge. The priesthood is not necessary to provide meaningful service opportunities. Other commendable organizations do so effectively to the benefit of many. So, how is the priesthood unique in blessing others? What is it that the priesthood can do for Heavenly Father's children that no other fraternal organization can?

The unique mission of the priesthood may be compared with the role of a rocket.[2] In this modern era of space exploration, a multistage rocket is an essential vehicle used to supply a space station or deliver a communications satellite into earth's orbit. The only purpose for these rockets is to deliver a payload, which is the valuable cargo the rocket transports. The payload's intrinsic value is fully realized only when it is delivered and functioning. The payload can be rendered inconsequential if it is not delivered to where it needs to be. One need not be a rocket scientist to appreciate that an expensive communications satellite is not useful in global communications if it is sitting in a warehouse. While a rocket might get a lot of attention as its fuel, in a controlled burn, generates hot gas to propel it into space, its purpose is simply as a payload delivery system.

The difficult part of rocketry is generating the appropriate thrust profile over time to lift the rocket and payload. Rocket propellant combustion is complex because it is dependent on many factors: temperature, pressure, surface area, particle mixing, and so on. The simple way of describing this is that one needs a "controlled burn." Small changes in environment can significantly alter a burn, so a rocket is an engineering feat that relies on redundancies, fail-safes, and wide margins. Because any additional weight to a rocket requires more fuel, additional features are not added randomly. All are considered carefully so they contribute to launch success. The bottom line is that a rocket is a complex piece of machinery. A rocket that does not deliver the payload where it needs to be is just a big, intricate, and costly firecracker.

As exciting as rockets and space may be, the most valuable

"payload" in the history of the world is not a satellite. It is "the love of God," His mercy and grace, which "is the most desirable above all things . . . and the most joyous to the soul" (1 Nephi 11:22–23). Forgiveness and salvation are made available to Heavenly Father's children because of the Savior's atoning sacrifice, which is made operative by means of the Holy Ghost. Without these blessings, creation's purpose is frustrated. Through them, Heavenly Father accomplishes His purposes: to save His children from physical and spiritual death and give them the kind of life He has, known as eternal life (see Doctrine and Covenants 14:7; 75:5; 88:4; 124:55; 131:5).

Through the Atonement of Jesus Christ, all who come to earth will be saved from physical death because resurrection is universally and unconditionally given. All may ultimately be saved from spiritual death, conditioned on obedience to the laws and ordinances of the gospel. But, for that to happen, the gospel with its laws and ordinances needs to be delivered to God's children. God's delivery system in this last and final dispensation is The Church of Jesus Christ of Latter-day Saints. This Church is His appointed vehicle—the rocket, so to speak.

The priesthood is tasked with delivering gospel covenants and ordinances to each man and woman. If priesthood holders fail to deliver this opportunity, they fail in their purpose. Therefore, Heavenly Father covenants with each Melchizedek Priesthood holder and teaches him the meaning of the covenant, to accomplish His work to bring His children safely back to their heavenly home. The covenant is made:

> . . . for the sake of the whole world.
> And the whole world lieth in sin, and groaneth under darkness and under the bondage of sin.
> And by this you may know they are under the bondage of sin, because they come not unto me [Jesus Christ].

For whoso cometh not unto me is under the bondage of sin. (Doctrine and Covenants 84:48–51)

The priesthood is on earth so that all may come unto Christ and receive saving and exalting ordinances. Through His Atonement, the bondage of sin may be removed. The priesthood holder can then stand with the Savior in fulfilling His mission:

> . . . to preach good tidings unto the meek . . . bind up the brokenhearted, to proclaim liberty to the captives, and the opening of the prison to them that are bound;
> . . . to comfort all that mourn;
> . . . to give unto them beauty for ashes, the oil of joy for mourning, the garment of praise for the spirit of heaviness. (Isaiah 61:1–3)

Fault analyses have sometimes identified minor defects in rockets that lead to mission failure. Brittle O-rings, sheared bolts, material fatigue, and even paint thickness can lead to combustion instabilities. Simply put, even seemingly minor components play a vital role. The priesthood holder has the incredible opportunity and responsibility to assist in making the Savior's atoning sacrifice available to the whole world as a latter-day rocket. All priesthood holders are vital, mission-critical components of the Lord's Atonement delivery system.

"Therefore, let every man stand in his own office, and labor in his own calling; and let not the head say unto the feet it hath no need of the feet; for without the feet how shall the body be able to stand? Also the body hath need of every member, that all may be edified together, that the system may be kept perfect" (Doctrine and Covenants 84:109–110).

I came to understand more fully our role in the Savior's work several years ago. One weekend, I was given two assignments. One was to create the first stake in a country. I was excited to be part of this historic event. The meetings were well attended by enthusiastic Saints. A wonderful stake presidency was called and sustained.

The second assignment came from the First Presidency. I was authorized to interview a young man and, if all was in order, restore his priesthood and temple blessings. This thirty-year-old man had joined the Church in his late teens. He served an honorable mission. But when he returned home, he lost his way and he lost his membership in the Church. After some years, "he came to himself" (Luke 15:17) and, with the help of loving priesthood leaders and kind members, he repented and was readmitted by baptism into the Church.

Approximately a year later, he had applied to have his priesthood and temple blessings restored. We set an appointment for the Saturday of the conference at 10:00 A.M. at the meetinghouse. When I arrived for the morning's earlier interviews, he was already there. He was so anxious to once again have the priesthood, he just could not wait.

During our interview, I showed him that President Thomas S. Monson had reviewed his application and authorized the interview just two days earlier. This stoic, handsome young man wept. As we continued, I told him that the date of our interview would have no meaning in his life. He looked puzzled. I informed him that after I restored his blessings, his membership record would show only his original baptism and confirmation dates, original priesthood ordination dates, and original endowment date. He again wept.

I asked him to read from the Doctrine and Covenants: "Behold, he who has repented of his sins, the same is forgiven, and I, the Lord, remember them no more. By this ye may know if a man repenteth of his sins—behold, he will confess them and forsake them" (Doctrine and Covenants 58:42–43).

He wept again.

Then, I placed my hands on his head, and, in the name of Jesus Christ, by the authority of the Melchizedek Priesthood, and with the authorization of the President of the Church, I restored his priesthood and temple blessings. The joy that came over us was profound. He knew he was once again worthy to hold the priesthood of God. He knew that the temple blessings he had received earlier were now fully operative. He had a bounce in his step and a radiant light about him. I was so proud of him and sensed how proud Heavenly Father was of him as well. I too wept with joy.

In my mind, the historic occasion of organizing the first stake in that country was overshadowed by the joy I felt in restoring the blessings to this young man. I have reflected on this experience and have come to realize that the purpose of organizing a stake, or indeed of using the priesthood of God in any way, is to assist Heavenly Father and Jesus Christ in their work, to redeem each of God's children. Like the rocket whose purpose is to deliver a payload, the priesthood is the vehicle that delivers the gospel of Jesus Christ, enabling all to choose to make covenants and receive ordinances. The "atoning blood of Christ" can thereby be applied in our lives as we receive Heavenly Father's promises and experience the sanctifying influence of the Holy Ghost (see Mosiah 4:2).

NOTES

1. See Stephen L Richards, in Conference Report, October 1938, 118.

2. See Dale G. Renlund, "The Priesthood and the Savior's Atoning Power," *Ensign*, November 2017.

Chapter 6

OATHS AND COVENANTS

God, willing more abundantly to shew
unto the heirs of promise the immutability of
his counsel, confirmed it by an oath.

—HEBREWS 6:16–17

Foundational to the priesthood is a covenant with God. The Melchizedek Priesthood has a covenant associated with it and is also accompanied by an oath. Oaths and covenants are pledges or vows that guarantee the future behavior of the participant. In the case of a priesthood holder, this covenant with God should change him forever. His priesthood covenant is something he should prepare for, learn about, clearly understand, and absolutely honor.

Oaths are intended to guide an individual's behavior. An account from the remarkable Lewis and Clark expedition is instructive. Meriwether Lewis and William Clark led forty-three others from St. Louis up the Missouri River on a 7,700-mile journey to the Pacific Ocean. In 1804, they encountered the Yankton Sioux, a group of Native Americans who had virtually no contact with the outside world. In his book *Undaunted Courage,* author Stephen

Ambrose provides a journal entry Captain Clark made on August 27, 1804, describing a group of braves: "They stayed by themselves, [are] fond of mirth, and assume a degree of superiority, [they are] stout likely fellows."

The reason they stood out was that they had made a vow "never to give back, let the danger be what it may." In other words, they would never retreat in battle. While their vow may not always have been strategically wise, their commitment to that vow made them different from the other tribe members.[1] They identified themselves with this pledge. In many ways, the pledge dictated their futures. If they failed to fulfill it, everyone would know.

The scriptures offer many examples of individuals whose lives were changed because they made a promise. Nephi, for instance, gave his word with an oath to Laban's servant Zoram that he need not fear, that he would be a free man if he went into the wilderness with Lehi's group. Because of the oath, Zoram took courage. After Zoram made an oath that he would stay with the group, the fears concerning him ceased (see 1 Nephi 4:32–37). Nephi's oath was an attestation that he would abide by his commitment to allow Zoram to be treated as a free man. Zoram's oath was a pledge that he would not seek to return to Jerusalem. Their standing with each other was established.

The importance of an oath was also shown when the Lamanite armies under their chief captain, Zerahemnah, were surrounded by Captain Moroni's army. The Lamanites were given an opportunity to leave if they would covenant not to fight anymore. Zerahemnah initially refused to take the oath because he knew he would break it (see Alma 44). Zerahemnah was asked to pledge his honor in the form of an oath. The purpose of the oath was to change Zerahemnah's behavior.

An oath had a similar impact on the people of Ammon in the

Book of Mormon. These people made a covenant to never take up arms again, even in their own defense. Their loyalty to the covenant defined them. On one occasion, when they were about to break that oath and fight in their own defense, their priesthood leader, Helaman—who himself would take up arms in the defense of the people—dissuaded them from doing so.

> They had taken an oath that they never would shed blood more. . . .
>
> But it came to pass that when they saw the danger, and the many afflictions and tribulations which the Nephites bore for them, they were moved with compassion and were desirous to take up arms in the defence of their country.
>
> But behold, as they were about to take their weapons of war, they were overpowered by the persuasions of Helaman and his brethren, for they were about to break the oath which they had made.
>
> And Helaman feared lest by so doing they should lose their souls. (Alma 53:11, 13–15)

How can breaking an oath, especially when it seems rational and expedient to do so, jeopardize one's soul? Because a covenant or an oath is a pledge of self. This concept is the central plot in a 1960 play, *A Man for All Seasons*.[2] In his preface to the play, playwright Robert Bolt indicates that some will wonder why he "takes as his hero a man who brings about his own death because he cannot put his hand on an old black book and tell an ordinary lie." The play is set in England when Henry VIII is on the throne. Sir Thomas More, a counselor to the king, has been loyal to Henry VIII. The king has proposed an act of succession that would allow him to separate from the Catholic church and become the head of the church in England. When Henry VIII requires his subjects to accept his proposal and swear allegiance to him, More refuses.

Sir Thomas More greatly loved the Catholic Church and was loyal to the Vatican Papacy. In the introduction to his play, Bolt answers the question as to why he would take such a man to be the hero. He says: "For this reason—a man takes an oath only when he wants to commit himself quite exceptionally to the statement, when he wants to make an identity between the truth of it and his own virtue; he offers himself as a guarantee. And, it works. There is a special kind of a shrug for a perjurer; we feel that a man has no self to commit, no guarantee to offer."

In the play, Sir Thomas More is jailed and his wife, daughter, and son-in-law come to visit. Sir Thomas's daughter, Meg, has agreed to try to persuade her father to *speak* the oath to the act of succession while in his heart *thinking* otherwise.

More explains to his daughter: "When a man takes an oath, Meg, he is holding his own self in his hands. Like water. And if he opens his fingers then—he needn't hope to find himself again. Some men aren't capable of this, but I'd be loathe to think your father one of them."

Sir Thomas More equates his oath with his identity and thereby defines himself. When a man makes this kind of promise, he is totally pledged to fulfilling it. Breaking the oath diminishes who he is, jeopardizing his very soul. The same is true for a priesthood holder who makes a covenant with God.

In Hebrews, Paul relates the historical precedent of God swearing oaths. Regarding the Abrahamic covenant, the scripture reads:

> For men verily swear by the greater: and an oath for confirmation is to them an end of all strife.
>
> Wherein God, willing more abundantly to shew unto the heirs of promise the *immutability* of his counsel, *confirmed it by an oath:*
>
> That by two immutable things, in which it was impossible

for God to lie, we might have a strong consolation, who have fled for refuge to lay hold upon the hope set before us:

Which hope we have as an *anchor of the soul, both sure and steadfast,* and which entereth into that within the veil;

Whither the forerunner is for us entered, even Jesus, made an high priest for ever after the order of Melchisedec. (Hebrews 6:16–20; emphasis added)

While an oath may be defined in various ways, in this context, it is a solemn witness or declaration that God sincerely intends to do what He says. He makes a solemn attestation of the inviolability of His promises.

The terms *oath* and *covenant* are sometimes used interchangeably, but they are not interchangeable when viewed in the context of the oath and covenant of the priesthood. The word *covenant* is of Latin origin, *con venire,* and literally means a "coming together." In the context of the priesthood, a "covenant" is a coming together or an agreement between God and man. It presupposes that God and man come together to make a contract, to agree on promises, stipulations, privileges, and responsibilities.

The Bible Dictionary entry for "Covenant" offers this insight: "It is important to notice that the two parties to the agreement do not stand in the relation of independent and equal contactors. God in His good pleasure fixes the terms, which man accepts." There is an inequality between the parties of the agreement. God initiates, determines the elements, and confirms His covenant. Priesthood holders are called on to accept the agreement as offered.

A covenant made in this manner is immutable and unchangeable. It anchors the soul; it creates a steadfast and sure foundation for future expectations. Jesus Christ became a high priest forever through a covenant with God the Father. God the Father then confirmed His covenant by an oath (see Psalm 110:1, 4).

Heavenly Father still uses covenants with priesthood holders today. But in the conferral of the Melchizedek Priesthood, He actually makes an oath to cement the relationship between Him and man. This covenant is so solemn that only when a priesthood holder is ready to commit himself to God and His work is he ready for the Melchizedek Priesthood.

NOTES

1. Stephen E. Ambrose, *Undaunted Courage: Meriwether Lewis, Thomas Jefferson, and the Opening of the American West* (1996), 161–63.

2. Robert Bolt, *A Man for All Seasons: A Play in Two Acts* (New York: Vintage International, 1990 edition), xiii–xiv; 140.

Chapter 7

The Oath and Covenant of the Priesthood

*All those who receive the priesthood,
receive this oath and covenant of my Father.*

—DOCTRINE AND COVENANTS 84:40

In association with the creation of the original Quorum of the Twelve Apostles in this dispensation in 1835, the Lord revealed the priesthood structure that is central in the restored Church.

There are, in the church, two priesthoods, namely, the Melchizedek and Aaronic, including the Levitical Priesthood.

Why the first is called the Melchizedek Priesthood is because Melchizedek was such a great high priest.

Before his day it was called the Holy Priesthood, after the Order of the Son of God.

But out of respect or reverence to the name of the Supreme Being, to avoid the too frequent repetition of his name, they, the church, in ancient days, called that priesthood after Melchizedek, or the Melchizedek Priesthood.

All other authorities or offices in the church are append-ages to this priesthood. (Doctrine and Covenants 107:1–5)

Every office in the Church originates with the Melchizedek Priesthood.[1] There is no other authority in the Church. The Joseph Smith Translation of the Bible explains that Melchizedek Priesthood is ancient, having no beginning or ending. In the account of Melchizedek's call to the priesthood, we read:

And thus, having been approved of God, [Melchizedek] was ordained an high priest after the order of the covenant which God made with Enoch,

It being after the order of the Son of God; which order came, not by man, nor the will of man; neither by father nor mother; neither by beginning of days nor end of years; but of God. (JST, Genesis 14:27–28)

Following a pattern our Heavenly Father established with Jesus Christ, those who receive the Melchizedek Priesthood and are faithful to their covenant retain it forever. Jesus Christ was told in the premortal existence that He would be a priest forever after the order of Melchizedek (see Psalm 110:4; JST, Hebrews 7:3). Melchizedek became part of that order. The Melchizedek Priesthood "continueth in the church of God in all generations, and is without beginning of days or end of years" (Doctrine and Covenants 84:17).

In contrast, the Aaronic Priesthood has a beginning. Follow-ing Israel's exodus from Egypt, Moses went up on Mount Sinai and communed with Jehovah. "Two tables of testimony, tables of stone, written with the finger of God" (Exodus 31:18), were given Moses. While waiting for Moses, Aaron, who was entreated by the people, made a golden calf, which Israel worshipped. When Moses returned from Mount Sinai, he broke the tables of stone. The ac-count continues:

"And the Lord said unto Moses . . . I will take away the priesthood out of their midst; therefore my holy order, and the ordinances thereof, shall not go before them; for my presence shall not go up in their midst, lest I destroy them. But I will give unto them the law as at the first, but it shall be after the law of a carnal commandment" (JST, Exodus 34:1–2; compare Exodus 34:1–2; Doctrine and Covenants 84:21–26).

The Melchizedek Priesthood was removed from the Israelites, and they were given the law of Moses. The Lord called Aaron, the brother of Moses, along with his sons and their direct descendants, to be the priests in a lesser priesthood called the Aaronic Priesthood (see Numbers 8). To assist priests in the Aaronic Priesthood, the Lord called other male members of the tribe of Levi, who were not descendants of Aaron, to carry out other priesthood assignments dealing with the portable tabernacle and the preparing and offering of sacrifices (see Numbers 3:5–13).

As concisely stated by the Lord in this dispensation: "And the Lord confirmed a priesthood also upon Aaron and his seed, throughout all their generations, which priesthood also continueth and abideth forever with the priesthood which is after the holiest order of God" (Doctrine and Covenants 84:18).

The Aaronic Priesthood began at the time of Moses, but it has no end because it abides forever with the Melchizedek Priesthood. The ongoing eternal nature of the Aaronic Priesthood is also seen in the promise given to Phinehas, the grandson of Aaron. In the Old Testament era, the posterity of Aaron held the Aaronic Priesthood. A plague afflicted the camp of Israel, at least in part because the Israelites worshipped false gods. In addition, an Israelite man brought a non-Israelite (Midianitish) woman into his tent and committed adultery. Phinehas took a javelin and killed both the man and the woman, ending the plague, which had already killed 24,000 people. The Lord told Moses to say the following to Phinehas: "Wherefore say, Behold, I give unto him my covenant of peace: And he shall have it, and his seed after him, even the covenant of an everlasting priesthood; because he was zealous for his God, and made an atonement for the children of Israel" (Numbers 25:12–13). Although the scriptures describe how the Aaronic Priesthood began, this passage of scripture indicates that the Aaronic Priesthood is everlasting or without end.

At the time of the Savior, leaders in the Church understood the difference between the two priesthoods. The Aaronic, encompassing the Levitical, is preparatory, and the ordinances thereof lead to the ordinances of the Melchizedek Priesthood, all of which are designed to focus individuals on the coming great atoning sacrifice of the Savior and to bring about the salvation of mankind.

The limitation of the lesser priesthood in accomplishing all of God's priesthood purposes is stated by Paul. If the lesser priesthood had been adequate for God's purposes, there would have been no need for a different priesthood. Paul says: "If therefore perfection were by the Levitical priesthood, (for under it the people received the law,) what further need was there that another priest should rise after the order of Melchisedec, and not be called after the order of Aaron?" (Hebrews 7:11).

Paul helps us understand that the Aaronic Priesthood came through the lineage of Levi and was called after the order of Aaron. This priesthood could not lead to perfection, and therefore the Melchizedek Priesthood was needed.

> For it is evident that our Lord sprang out of Juda; of which tribe Moses spake nothing concerning priesthood.
>
> And it is yet far more evident: for that after the similitude of Melchisedec there ariseth another priest,

Who is made, not after the law of a carnal commandment, but after the power of an endless life.

For he testifieth, Thou art a priest for ever after the order
of Melchisedec. (Hebrews 7:14–17)

Jesus Christ was of the tribe of Judah, not a Levite, and therefore a priest after a different order, that of Melchizedek. Melchizedek
Priesthood keys authorize covenants and ordinances that are needed
for eternal life. Jesus, the prototypical high priest of the Melchizedek
Priesthood, came with this authority.

THE AARONIC PRIESTHOOD COVENANT

Covenants and promises accompany the conferral of both the
Aaronic and Melchizedek Priesthoods. As seen with Phinehas,
a priesthood covenant is associated with the Aaronic Priesthood (see
Numbers 25:10–13). A covenant of an everlasting priesthood and a
covenant of peace were given Phinehas. These covenants are still associated with the Aaronic Priesthood (see Nehemiah 13:29).

As with all covenants, the blessings of the Aaronic Priesthood
come through righteousness and faithfulness. Phinehas demonstrated his faithfulness by siding with God and reconciling Israel
to Him. Phinehas reconciling Israel to God foreshadows that the
Aaronic Priesthood would hold the keys of the gospel of repentance
(see Doctrine and Covenants 13:1).

When the Aaronic Priesthood is conferred, the recipient covenants to:

- Accept the obligation to help individuals become reconciled
  to God (covenant of peace; see Numbers 25:12–13);
- Be free from iniquity (see Nehemiah 13:29; Malachi 2:2–9);
- Lead others from iniquity (see Ezekiel 34:2–6; Doctrine
  and Covenants 20:46–59); and

- Prepare to receive the Melchizedek Priesthood (see Hebrews 7; Doctrine and Covenants 84:33–40).

These sacred responsibilities are fulfilled by teaching, baptizing, watching over and strengthening the Church, visiting members, and inviting all to come unto Christ.

In return, God promises:

- Hope (see Hebrews 7:19);
- Forgiveness (see Doctrine and Covenants 84:27);
- Keys for the ministering of angels (see Doctrine and Covenants 84:26); and
- Keys for the preparatory gospel (see Doctrine and Covenants 84:26).

These blessings are profound. Consequently, Heavenly Father attaches dire penalties for failure to live up to priesthood covenants. For instance, Malachi describes the consequences of breaking this covenant anciently:

> If ye will not hear, and if ye will not lay it to heart, to give glory unto my name, saith the Lord of hosts, I will even send a curse upon you, and I will curse your blessings: yea, I have cursed them already, because ye do not lay it to heart.
>
> Behold, I will corrupt your seed, and spread dung upon your faces, even the dung of your solemn feasts. . . .
>
> And ye shall know that I have sent this commandment unto you, that my covenant might be with Levi, saith the Lord of hosts.
>
> My covenant was with him of life and peace; and I gave them to him for the fear wherewith he feared me, and was afraid before my name.
>
> The law of truth was in his mouth, and iniquity was not found in his lips: he walked with me in peace and equity, and did turn many away from iniquity.

For the priest's lips should keep knowledge, and they should seek the law at his mouth: for he is the messenger of the Lord of hosts.

But ye are departed out of the way; ye have caused many to stumble at the law; ye have corrupted the covenant of Levi, saith the Lord of hosts. (Malachi 2:2–8)

One of the glorious tasks of the Aaronic Priesthood is to turn individuals away from wickedness by teaching them the gospel of repentance. To accomplish this, the priesthood holder must be virtuous, not self-serving, and take seriously his covenant with God. If the priesthood holder does not do his part, priesthood labors come to naught.

It is obvious that a man can break the priesthood covenant by being disobedient, but there is a second way. President Spencer W. Kimball said, "One breaks the priesthood covenant by transgressing commandments—but also by leaving undone his duties. Accordingly, to break this covenant one needs only to do nothing."[2]

THE MELCHIZEDEK PRIESTHOOD COVENANT

A covenant is also associated with the Melchizedek Priesthood. This covenant was established with Enoch, Melchizedek, and Jesus Christ (see JST, Genesis 14:27, 33; Hebrews 7:14–17), and with everyone who is ordained to the Melchizedek Priesthood (see Doctrine and Covenants 84:33–40, 48).

A Melchizedek Priesthood holder covenants to fulfill all that is included in the Aaronic Priesthood covenants and, after receiving the Melchizedek Priesthood, to magnify his priesthood calling.

Specifically, a Melchizedek Priesthood holder covenants to:

- Give diligent heed to the words of eternal life so that he can live by every word that proceeds from the mouth of God (see Doctrine and Covenants 84:43–44);

- Take the testimony of the Savior to the world (see Doctrine and Covenants 84:61–62);
- Not boast of himself (see Doctrine and Covenants 84:73);
- Become the Savior's friend and trust Him like a friend (see Doctrine and Covenants 84:63, 77–88); and
- Fulfill responsibilities associated with the Abrahamic covenant (see Doctrine and Covenants 84:34).

God promises great blessings to the Melchizedek Priesthood holder who keeps his priesthood covenants. Early in this dispensation, the Lord said:

> For whoso is faithful unto the obtaining these two priesthoods of which I have spoken [Aaronic and Melchizedek], and the magnifying their calling, are sanctified by the Spirit unto the renewing of their bodies.
>
> They become the sons of Moses and of Aaron and the seed of Abraham, and the church and kingdom, and the elect of God.
>
> And also all they who receive this priesthood receive me, saith the Lord;
>
> For he that receiveth my servants receiveth me;
>
> And he that receiveth me receiveth my Father;
>
> And he that receiveth my Father receiveth my Father's kingdom; therefore all that my Father hath shall be given unto him.
>
> And this is according to the oath and covenant which belongeth to the priesthood.
>
> Therefore, all those who receive the priesthood, receive this oath and covenant of my Father, which he cannot break, neither can it be moved. (Doctrine and Covenants 84:33–40)

Specifically, God covenants that the Melchizedek Priesthood holder will:

- Become an heir to the priesthood line of Moses and Aaron;[3]
- Become an heir to the Abrahamic covenant (see Doctrine and Covenants 84:34);
- Receive keys to the mysteries of God's kingdom and the knowledge of God (see Doctrine and Covenants 84:19);
- Be enabled to become perfect (see Hebrews 7);
- Receive eternal life (see Doctrine and Covenants 84:38);
- Be befriended by the Savior and provided all that is needed to accomplish the work of salvation and exaltation (see Doctrine and Covenants 84:42, 77–88);
- Have power, by faith, to do all things, even to direct the elements, to put at defiance the rulers of the earth, and to stand in the presence of God (see JST, Genesis 14:26–37);
- Be sanctified by the Spirit to the renewing of his body (see Doctrine and Covenants 84:33); and
- Become a joint-heir with Jesus Christ to everything that He receives from Heavenly Father (see Doctrine and Covenants 84:38).

We can have absolute confidence that Heavenly Father will keep His promises. To each man who receives the Melchizedek Priesthood, God affirms His covenant with an oath. The scriptures indicate that this oath pertains to the Melchizedek Priesthood and that it is God who swears with an oath as part of this covenant.[4] In this unique situation involving His divine power and authority, God employs the most forceful and unequivocal language He can to assure us of the binding and unalterable character of His promises.

And thus, having been approved of God, [Melchizedek] was ordained an high priest after the order of the covenant which God made with Enoch,

It being after the order of the Son of God . . .

And it was delivered unto men by the calling of his [God's] own voice, according to his own will . . .

For God having sworn unto Enoch and unto his seed *with an oath by himself;* that every one being ordained after this order and calling should have power . . .

. . . to do all things according to his [God's] will. (JST, Genesis 14:27–31; emphasis added)

Similarly, our Heavenly Father declared with an oath that Jesus Christ would be a priest forever after the order of Melchizedek: "The Lord said unto my Lord, Sit thou at my right hand, until I make thine enemies thy footstool. *The Lord hath sworn,* and will not repent, Thou art a priest for ever after the order of Melchizedek" (Psalm 110:1, 4; emphasis added).

The Apostle Paul also taught that the higher priesthood, the Melchizedek Priesthood, was associated with an oath. The lesser priesthood, he says, administered the law of carnal commandments. He says:

For the law was administered *without an oath* and made nothing perfect, but was only the bringing in of a better hope; by the which we draw nigh unto God.

Inasmuch as this high priest [Jesus Christ] was *not without an oath* [in other words, with an oath], by so much was Jesus made the surety of a better testament.

(For those priests [priests in the Aaronic and Levitical Priesthood] were made *without an oath;* but this [the Melchizedek Priesthood] *with an oath* by him that said unto him, The Lord sware and will not repent, Thou art a priest forever after the order of Melchizedek;) (JST, Hebrews 7:19–21; emphasis added)

Through these scriptures we understand that the Aaronic Priesthood is associated with a covenant but involves no oath. The Aaronic Priesthood was a means of ushering in the "better hope," the hope that comes from the Melchizedek Priesthood.[5] The ultimate high priest, Jesus Christ, is the "better hope."

As with the Aaronic Priesthood, Heavenly Father declares severe consequences for breaking and altogether turning from the "oath and covenant which belongeth to the priesthood" (Doctrine and Covenants 84:39). "But whoso breaketh this covenant after he hath received it, and altogether turneth therefrom, shall not have forgiveness of sins in this world nor in the world to come" (Doctrine and Covenants 84:41).

Just as we can trust His promised blessings, we can trust God's promised punishment. The severity of the punishment could lead one to not want to enter the covenant in the first place. But, there are also consequences for not entering the priesthood covenant. "And wo unto all those who come *not* unto this priesthood which ye have received . . ." (Doctrine and Covenants 84:42; emphasis added).

Through Melchizedek Priesthood conferral, God invites men on earth to participate with Him in His great and glorious purpose. Those who choose not to help Him, either after making the covenant or by refusing to accept it, are denied the great and glorious blessings He has sworn to bestow. Priesthood holders in the Church are obligated to understand and honor the priesthood covenants they have made.

NOTES

1. The scriptural references to priesthood covenants or oaths are found in the following scriptures. These references do not pertain to the Abrahamic Covenant.
   • JST, Genesis 14:26–37
   • Numbers 25:10–13
   • Nehemiah 13:29

- Psalm 110:1, 4
- Malachi 2:2–8
- Hebrews 7:3 (JST), 7, 11, 14–17, 19–21 (JST)
- Doctrine and Covenants 84:5–42

2. *The Teachings of Spencer W. Kimball,* edited by Edward L. Kimball (1982), 497.

3. The Melchizedek Priesthood line of authority as it pertains to Moses is found in Doctrine and Covenants 84:6–17, 32–34.

4. There is no scriptural reference or account of the recipient swearing an oath as he makes the Melchizedek Priesthood covenant. In each scriptural instance (JST, Genesis 14:27–31; Psalm 110:1, 4; Hebrews 7:21; Doctrine and Covenants 84:40), it is God who swears an oath as He makes the covenant with the recipient. However, some Church leaders may have suggested that the recipient swears an oath. President Joseph Fielding Smith said, "There is no exaltation in the kingdom of God without the fullness of the priesthood, and every man who receives the Melchizedek Priesthood does so with an oath and a covenant that he shall be exalted. The covenant on man's part is that he will magnify his calling in the priesthood, and that he will live by every word that proceedeth forth from the mouth of God, and that he will keep the commandments" (in Conference Report, April 1970, 58–59). President Gordon B. Hinckley said, "In the very process of accepting ordination he enters into an oath and covenant between himself and his God" ("Only upon Principles of Righteousness," *Ensign,* September 1992). President Russell M. Nelson said, "Those who receive the Melchizedek Priesthood are under solemn oath and covenant to 'live by every word that proceedeth forth from the mouth of God' (Doctrine and Covenants 84:44)" ("Keys of the Priesthood, *Ensign,* November 1987). President Spencer W. Kimball unambiguously said, "Now you made an oath, when you received the priesthood. You made an oath, and you cannot with impunity ignore that oath" (in Scandinavian Area Conference, August 1974, 99–100). It would be inconsistent for man to swear an oath, since the Savior said: "Again, ye have heard that it hath been said by them of old time, Thou shalt not forswear thyself, but shalt perform unto the Lord thine oaths: But I say unto you, Swear not at all; neither by heaven; for it is God's throne: Nor by the earth; for it is his footstool: neither by Jerusalem; for it is the city of the great King. Neither shalt thou swear by thy head, because thou canst not make one hair white or black. But let your communication be, Yea, yea; Nay, nay: for whatsoever is more than these cometh of evil" (Matthew 5:33–37).

5. See Bruce R. McConkie, "The Doctrine of the Priesthood," *Ensign,* May 1982. Elder McConkie further taught: "And so the Lord uses the most powerful and emphatic language known to the human tongue to show their importance and immutability. That is to say, the Lord swears with an oath in his own name, because he can swear by no greater, that everyone who keeps

the covenant made in connection with the Melchizedek Priesthood shall inherit, receive, and possess all things in his everlasting kingdom, and shall be a joint-heir with that Lord who is his Only Begotten. God swore with an oath that Christ would be exalted [Psalm 110:4], and he swears anew, at the time each of us receives the Melchizedek Priesthood, that we will have a like exaltation if we are true and faithful in all things" (ibid.).

Chapter 8

COMMANDMENTS OF THE MELCHIZEDEK PRIESTHOOD COVENANT

It is expedient that I give unto you this commandment.

—DOCTRINE AND COVENANTS 84:77

All blessings are conditioned on keeping commandments. The Lord said: "There is a law, irrevocably decreed in heaven before the foundations of this world, upon which all blessings are predicated—and when we obtain any blessing from God, it is by obedience to that law upon which it is predicated" (Doctrine and Covenants 130:20–21).

The blessings of the oath and covenant of the priesthood are conditioned upon obeying the commandment to magnify one's calling. "For whoso is faithful unto the obtaining these two priesthoods of which I have spoken, and the *magnifying their calling*, are sanctified by the Spirit unto the renewing of their bodies" (Doctrine and Covenants 84:33; emphasis added).

How does one magnify a Melchizedek Priesthood calling? We are not left to wonder; the Lord provides at least one answer in the form of four commandments found in Doctrine and Covenants 84, each of which is preceded by a phrase designating it as a commandment.

COMMANDMENT 1: *Pay attention to the words of eternal life because you need to live by every word that comes from God*

The first commandment is: "And *I now give unto you a commandment* to beware concerning yourselves, to give diligent heed to the words of eternal life. For you shall live by every word that proceedeth forth from the mouth of God" (Doctrine and Covenants 84:43–44; emphasis added).

This commandment informs the priesthood holder to carefully pay attention to every word that comes from God and to live by those words. The words of God are found in at least five sources, as illustrated by the following experience.

As an Area Seventy, I was training a new stake presidency with a member of the Presidency of the Seventy. He instructed the brethren to consider their stewardship as a field. Each side of the field is bordered by either the scriptures, handbooks, the words of living prophets and apostles, or file leaders. Within the field, he added a fifth source, the Holy Ghost. To illustrate the point, he drew the figure below on a blackboard.

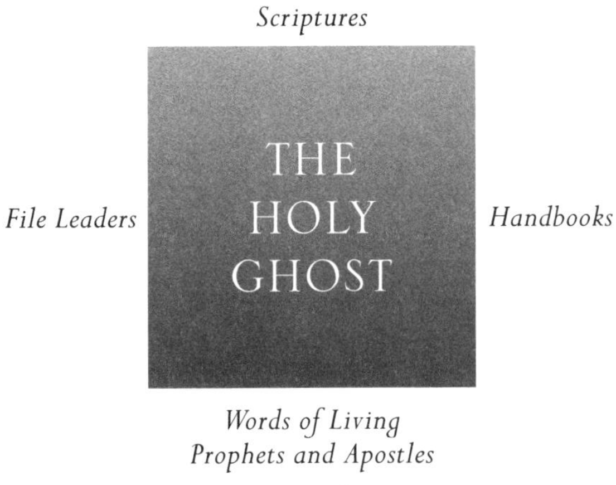

Scriptures

File Leaders   THE HOLY GHOST   *Handbooks*

Words of Living Prophets and Apostles

Figure 2.

Scriptures represent the word of the Lord to past generations, through deceased prophets. The scriptures are relevant to today's challenges. When a priesthood holder faces a challenge, he should ask himself, "What in the scriptures will help me know what to do?" The scriptures provide answers to most questions.

Handbooks contain the doctrine, policies, and procedures for the Church. They constitute a library and a reference guide. President James E. Faust said, "The handbooks are no more and no less than the collective wisdom of the First Presidency and the Twelve."[1] Handbooks can help us know how to live by every word that comes from God. Like the scriptures, handbooks provide direction from Heavenly Father's anointed leaders and can be used to address a priesthood challenge.

Adding to scriptures and handbooks, a priesthood holder relies on the words of living prophets and apostles. Their words are readily available from general conference addresses, Church magazines, and other Church publications. They have an added imprimatur when the First Presidency and Quorum of the Twelve speak unitedly. "The Family: A Proclamation to the World"[2] and "The Living Christ: The Testimony of the Apostles—The Church of Jesus Christ of Latter-day Saints"[3] are examples. Through these means, we can discern the doctrine of the Church and the word of the Lord.

In His introduction to the Doctrine and Covenants, the Lord states:

> Search these commandments, for they are true and faithful, and the prophecies and promises which are in them shall all be fulfilled.
>
> What I the Lord have spoken, I have spoken, and I excuse not myself; and though the heavens and the earth pass away, my word shall not pass away, but shall all be fulfilled, *whether by mine own voice or by the voice of my servants, it is the same.*" (Doctrine and Covenants 1:37–38; emphasis added)

This is so because the Lord said: "And whatsoever they shall speak when moved upon by the Holy Ghost shall be scripture, shall be the will of the Lord, shall be the mind of the Lord, shall be the word of the Lord, shall be the voice of the Lord, and the power of God unto salvation" (Doctrine and Covenants 68:4).

After evaluating God's words from scriptures, handbooks, and living apostles and prophets, one follows the counsel received from those set apart to lead. These are often referred to as file leaders. File leaders usually hold priesthood keys and preside over the priesthood holder.

For example, an elders quorum president's file leader is the stake president, who holds keys of presidency. The counselors in a stake presidency also preside over the elders quorum president through keys delegated by the stake president for tasks and assignments. A priesthood holder who treats his stewardship as being framed by scriptures, handbooks, living prophets and apostles, and file leaders is well on his way to fulfilling his responsibility.

Governing all a priesthood holder's actions is the Holy Ghost. The Holy Ghost guides the priesthood holder *within the framework* established by the other four sources. "Notwithstanding those things which are written, it always has been given to the elders of my church from the beginning, and ever shall be, to conduct all meetings as they are directed and guided by the Holy Spirit" (Doctrine and Covenants 46:2).

This verse suggests that fulfilling a priesthood responsibility is much more nuanced than implementing a handbook. The Holy Ghost must always be sought if a person is to accomplish a calling in the Lord's way. Rigidly following handbook instruction can lead to a wrong result if the Spirit is ignored. It is easier to obtain revelation regarding the work when one is familiar with handbooks, scriptures, the words of living prophets and apostles, and direction from file leaders.

At our daughter's university graduation, we attended a speech by a famed NASA astronaut. The distinguished and experienced astronaut said that at NASA there was a saying: "There are two ways to cause a mission to fail. The first is to not explicitly follow all established rules, policies, and procedures. And the second way is to explicitly follow all established rules policies and procedures." Why? Implementing a procedural handbook without taking into account changing and frequently unanticipated circumstances is foolish and can cause mission failure.

The same is true for a priesthood holder. Handbooks alone are not sufficient. The Holy Ghost is the source of understanding the words of eternal life. Through the Holy Ghost, the scriptures, handbooks, words of living apostles and prophets, and directions from file leaders are applied. A priesthood holder can be assured that giving heed to God's word and the Holy Ghost will provide a foundation for magnifying his calling.

COMMANDMENT 2: *Share the fulness of the gospel of Jesus Christ with everyone*

The second commandment associated with the Melchizedek Priesthood covenant is to bear testimony to all the world of those things that are communicated to the priesthood holder. In other words, doing missionary work and sharing the fulness of the gospel of Jesus Christ with everyone is the responsibility of every priesthood holder.

> For I will forgive you of your sins with this *commandment*—that you remain steadfast in your minds in solemnity and the spirit of prayer, in bearing testimony to all the world of those things which are communicated unto you.

Therefore, go ye into all the world; and unto whatsoever place ye cannot go ye shall send, that the testimony may go from you into all the world unto every creature.

And as I said unto mine apostles, even so I say unto you, for you are mine apostles, even God's high priests; ye are they whom my Father hath given me; ye are my friends;

Therefore, as I said unto mine apostles I say unto you again, that . . . every soul who believeth on your words, and is baptized by water for the remission of sins, shall receive the Holy Ghost. (Doctrine and Covenants 84:61–64; emphasis added)

Although the Lord uses the term *apostle* in these verses, he is speaking to all those ordained to the Melchizedek Priesthood. At the time of the revelation in 1832, the Quorum of the Twelve Apostles had not yet been organized and would not be until 1835. The word *apostle* comes from the Greek, meaning "one sent forth."[4] Thus, all missionaries who are called, set apart, and sent forth away from their homes to preach the gospel share in an apostolic calling.[5]

The commandment speaks of bearing testimony to the world of those things that are received. When we follow this commandment, others are baptized and receive the Holy Ghost. It seems most probable that this commandment relates to being a missionary, to "invite others to come unto Christ by helping them receive the restored gospel through faith in Jesus Christ and His Atonement, repentance, baptism, receiving the gift of the Holy Ghost, and enduring to the end."[6]

Of course, this commandment is not fulfilled only by full-time, set-apart missionaries. A Primary teacher, a Sunday School teacher, or a temple and family history consultant, for example, called and set apart by those who hold the priesthood, has the authority to fulfill this commandment. As men and women bear testimony and invite others to come unto Christ, they follow this commandment.

God says He will forgive us our sins as we comply with this commandment. The sins that are to be forgiven may be those of ignoring the Book of Mormon and prior revelations (see Doctrine and Covenants 84:54–61). However, this promise may be even more expansive because there is no activity, other than baptism, that is more closely associated with the promise of forgiveness of sin than that of missionary work.[7]

COMMANDMENT 3: *Do not boast of miracles in your priesthood ministry*

As a priesthood holder fulfills the commandment to preach the gospel, he will witness wondrous things, even miracles. Those who are sent forth with apostolic authority will, in the name of the Savior, cast out devils, heal the sick, open the eyes of the blind, unstop the ears of the deaf, and cause the dumb to speak. The priesthood holder may even be protected from harmful events, those occurring naturally and those caused by others who wish to cause harm (see Doctrine and Covenants 84:65–72).

A priesthood holder might feel proud about his role in wondrous events. The Lord anticipated these natural tendencies and gave a third commandment: "But *a commandment I give unto them,* that they shall not boast themselves of these things, neither speak them before the world; for these things are given unto you for your profit and for salvation" (Doctrine and Covenants 84:73; emphasis added).

In short, priesthood holders should not boast of the miracles seen in their priesthood ministry. Neither should they share them widely or with nonbelievers. Why? There seem to be at least two reasons for this commandment.

First is the corrupting power of personal pride. We know that when we seek to gratify our pride or our vain ambition, priesthood power itself is ineffectual. When we seek the honors of men, priesthood changes to priestcraft. Priestcraft occurs as a priesthood holder sets himself up as "a light unto the world" to get personal gain and to receive the praise of the world instead of seeking the welfare of the Church (2 Nephi 26:29). Priestcraft also occurs when a priesthood holder seeks to become popular (see Alma 1:3).

Boasting is a serious sin for a priesthood holder. Remember Alma and his need to correct Corianton? The first correction he mentions is Corianton's boastfulness: "Now this is what I have against thee; thou didst go on unto boasting in thy strength and thy wisdom" (Alma 39:2).

Boasting of one's strength ignores the real source of a priesthood holder's strength: God. When he takes credit for God's work, he becomes self-sufficient, self-centered, and self-aggrandizing. While the priesthood holder is blessed as he performs his priesthood labors, the primary reason the priesthood is on earth is to bless others.

Second, sharing miracles with nonbelievers does not build faith. As stated in the Bible Dictionary, "Faith is kindled by hearing the testimony of those who have faith (Rom. 10:14–17). Miracles do not produce faith, but strong faith is developed by obedience to the gospel of Jesus Christ; in other words, faith comes by righteousness, although miracles often confirm one's faith."[8] Miracles by themselves do not produce faith; therefore, speaking widely about them can diminish their significance, leaving special experiences open for ridicule, speculation, and disregard. A long-lasting change of heart comes not from seeing or hearing about miracles but by experiencing a changed heart. Part of magnifying the priesthood includes feeling a quiet gratitude for God's allowing us to participate in His mighty work.

COMMANDMENT 4: *Become the Savior's friend*

The fourth commandment associated with magnifying one's calling in the priesthood is an all-encompassing and intimate invitation: "And again I say unto you, my friends, for from hence-forth I shall call you friends, it is expedient that *I give unto you this commandment,* that ye become even as my friends in days when I was with them, traveling to preach the gospel in my power" (Doctrine and Covenants 84:77; emphasis added).

The commandment, stated imperatively, is: "Be My friend." The Savior told His Apostles of old: "Ye are my friends, if ye do whatso-ever I command you. Henceforth I call you not servants; for the ser-vant knoweth not what his lord doeth: but I have called you friends; for all things that I have heard of my Father I have made known unto you" (John 15:14–15).

The way to become His friend today is no different than in days of old. It starts with a commitment to keep His commandments. The Savior cannot share all that Heavenly Father has communicated to Him unless the priesthood holder is willing to completely align his will with God's. Once a priesthood holder is so aligned and will-ing to consecrate his life to the Savior, his standing with the Savior changes. He is not simply a disciple; he is certainly not a hireling or an evangelical mercenary. He is the Savior's friend, and the Savior will be his friend—but not an ordinary friend. He is a friend who carries burdens, cares for needs, and sustains a priesthood holder on His errand.

The Savior says to the priesthood holder that he will receive help in teaching the gospel: "Neither take ye thought beforehand what ye shall say; but treasure up in your minds continually the words of life, and it shall be given you in the very hour that portion that shall be meted unto every man" (Doctrine and Covenants 84:85).

In addition, the priesthood holder is not left to labor alone. The Lord Himself will work with him just as a friend would. In the al-legory of the olive tree, the Lord of the vineyard, who represents the Lord, joins the priesthood holders in the vineyard. "And it came to pass that the servants did go and labor with their mights; and the Lord of the vineyard labored also with them; and they did obey the commandments of the Lord of the vineyard in all things" (Jacob 5:72).

Through Joseph Smith, the Lord revealed: "And whoso receiveth you, there I will be also, for I will go before your face. I will be on your right hand and on your left, and my Spirit shall be in your hearts, and mine angels round about you, to bear you up" (Doctrine and Covenants 84:88).

Our Friend is in the vineyard laboring today, supporting the priesthood holder in his responsibility. He has prepared the way over decades for those priesthood holders who trust the Lord as a friend. Friends trust each other. They work together to build God's kingdom.

God has given man the Melchizedek Priesthood, with an oath and covenant, and instructed him how to magnify this priesthood. He promises great blessing to those who heed the words of eternal life, bear testimony to the world, do not boast of themselves, and become His friends. Armed with such knowledge and promises, it is time for priesthood holders to go to work.

God implores: "Therefore, let every man stand in his own office, and labor in his own calling" (Doctrine and Covenants 84:109).

NOTES

1. James E. Faust, Area Authority/General Authority Training, 2002.

2. "The Family: A Proclamation to the World," *Ensign,* November 2010. This proclamation was read by President Gordon B. Hinckley as part of his message at the General Relief Society Meeting held September 23, 1995, in Salt Lake City, Utah.

3. "The Living Christ: The Testimony of the Apostles—The Church of Jesus Christ of Latter-day Saints," First Presidency letter, December 10, 1999. See *Doctrine and Covenants and Church History Seminary Teacher Resource Manual* (2001), 282–83.

4. See Guide to the Scriptures, "Apostle."

5. This apostolic calling is denoted by using the lowercase "a," whereas the Melchizedek Priesthood office of Apostle is usually capitalized.

6. *Preach My Gospel: A Guide to Missionary Service* (2004), 1.

7. Sample scriptures that promise forgiveness of sins for those who engage in missionary work: Doctrine and Covenants 4:2,4; 6:3; 12:3; 14:3; 21:9; 31:5; 36:1; 60:7; 62:3; Psalm 40:8–13.

8. Bible Dictionary, "Faith."

Section Two

DOCTRINE

of the

PRIESTHOOD

Chapter 9

PRINCIPLE #1

THE RIGHTS OF THE PRIESTHOOD
ARE GOVERNED BY PRINCIPLES
OF RIGHTEOUSNESS

*The rights of the priesthood are inseparably
connected with the powers of heaven.*
—DOCTRINE AND COVENANTS 121:36

The doctrine of the priesthood includes the set of principles governing its use. The rights of the priesthood refer to the privileges
and entitlements that are accorded to the priesthood holder. But the
overriding principle is righteousness. As the Lord has revealed: "The
rights of the priesthood are inseparably connected with the powers
of heaven, and . . . the powers of heaven cannot be controlled nor
handled only upon the principles of righteousness" (Doctrine and
Covenants 121:36).

How could it be otherwise? God embodies all righteousness, and
to use the "powers of heaven," a priesthood holder must diligently
strive to be like God. Although no priesthood holder is perfect, it is
impossible to conceive that the priesthood can be used for unrighteous pursuits. The revelation continues: "But when we undertake
to cover our sins, or to gratify our pride, our vain ambition, or to

exercise control or dominion or compulsion upon the souls of the children of men, in any degree of unrighteousness, behold, the heavens withdraw themselves; the Spirit of the Lord is grieved; and when it is withdrawn, Amen to the priesthood or the authority of that man" (Doctrine and Covenants 121:37).

Just as life on earth is connected to physical laws, the priesthood is governed by eternal laws. Violating physical laws without considering the consequences is reckless. Jumping off a building and thinking that gravity will not exert its predictable effect is as foolish as thinking that priesthood can be used contrary to its governing laws.

An event from the early seventeenth century in Sweden illustrates the consequences of ignoring physical laws.

In the early 1600s, Sweden was a world power because of its navy. Its domination was fueled by natural resources of oak, hemp, and pitch that were critical for shipbuilding. Sweden's king, Gustav II Adolf, commissioned a warship, the *Vasa,* that represented a substantial outlay of resources, particularly the oak from which the vessel was being built. Oak was so valuable that cutting down an oak tree without authorization was a capital offense. Gustav Adolf closely oversaw the construction process to ensure that the *Vasa* would fully realize his expectations as his flagship.

After construction began, Gustav Adolf wanted the *Vasa* to be larger. Because the width supports had already been built from precious oak, the king directed the builders to increase the ship's length without increasing its width. Although the shipwrights knew that doing so would compromise *Vasa's* seaworthiness, they were hesitant to tell the king something he did not want to hear. So, they complied. Gustav Adolf also insisted that this ship should have more than the customary single deck of guns; he wanted cannons on three decks, with the heaviest cannons on the upper deck. Again, against their better judgment, the shipwrights complied.

Over the course of several years, shipwrights, carpenters, rope makers, and others worked diligently to build the *Vasa*. Over one thousand oak trees were used to complete the ship. It had sixty-four cannons, and masts taller than 150 feet. To give the ship the opulence befitting a king's flagship, several hundred gilded and painted sculptures were added.

On August 10, 1628, the *Vasa* began its maiden voyage. Before countless spectators, the ship left its mooring immediately below the Royal Castle in Stockholm. After being pulled along by anchors for the first several hundred feet, the *Vasa* left the shelter of the harbor. A strong wind entered its sails, and the ship began to tip. The *Vasa* righted herself slightly, but only temporarily. Before long, as recorded by an observer, "she heeled right over and water gushed in through the gun ports until she slowly went to the bottom under sail, pennants and all."[1] The *Vasa*'s maiden voyage covered about 4,200 feet.

The *Vasa* rested at the bottom of the Gulf of Bothnia until it was recovered three centuries later, in 1961. It was successfully raised from the seabed and towed back to Stockholm. Today, the *Vasa* rests in a temperature- and humidity-controlled museum in Djurgården, an island in central Stockholm.

Despite the *Vasa*'s magnificent appearance, the ship was not seaworthy. The alterations in its construction resulted in insufficient lateral stability to enable safe seafaring. Gustav Adolf's desire for an extravagant status symbol ruined the design of what would have been a serviceable sailing vessel, the mightiest warship of its time. The story of the *Vasa* stands as a reminder that no matter how powerful a king may be, he is not more powerful than the laws of physics.

In a similar way, priesthood is governed by eternal laws, including principles of righteousness, that cannot be ignored without disastrous consequences. A priesthood holder must comply with the laws that govern the use of the priesthood or he will fail in his service. When used in a self-serving way, priesthood becomes priestcraft, and priesthood authority is extinguished.

God knows that His priesthood is given to imperfect men. However, even imperfect men can exercise the priesthood with good effect if they do so in accordance with correct principles. A priesthood holder must forever try to be righteous. He must be humble, meek, and submissive. Such an imperfect man will, by the grace of God, bring to pass good works. Even a perfect man, if one existed, could not exercise the priesthood for improper, unrighteous purposes.[2]

NOTES

1. The story of the *Vasa* has been recounted in numerous places. See, for instance, www.Vasamuseet.se for history and other links.

2. The Book of Mormon describes several instances when individuals attempted to use religion to acquire personal gain, praise, or glory (see 1 Nephi 22:23; 2 Nephi 26:29; 2 Nephi 27:16; Alma 1:3, 16; Helaman 7:5). Each time, the man misusing power or influence was condemned.

Chapter 10

Principle #2
The Proper Exercise
of Priesthood Is Learned

*It is the nature and disposition of almost
all men . . . to exercise unrighteous dominion.*
—Doctrine and Covenants 121:39

The use of the priesthood does not come naturally to most men.
A familiar scripture associated with the priesthood makes this
penetrating point:

"We have learned by sad experience that it is the nature and
disposition of almost all men, as soon as they get a little authority,
as they suppose, they will immediately begin to exercise unrighteous
dominion" (Doctrine and Covenants 121:39).

Correct use of the priesthood is not instinctive. It is difficult
to master and takes time. This challenge is not new. The Savior
struggled with His Apostles in ancient days to help them understand
how to use priesthood authority correctly. Recall that two brothers,
James and John, asked the Savior if they could become the premier
Apostles. They each requested to be seated beside Jesus after His
glorification. The response of the other ten Apostles was predictable:

"And when the ten heard it, they began to be much displeased with James and John" (Mark 10:41).

No surprise there. As James and John jockeyed for position in the Quorum of the Twelve Apostles, the others became unhappy. The brothers' pride and their desire to gratify their ambition resulted in resentment and disunity.

The Savior then taught a remarkable principle: Priesthood patterns are not learned by copying examples in the world. Priesthood holders must learn the Savior's way.

> But Jesus called them to him, and saith unto them, Ye know that they which are accounted to rule over the Gentiles exercise lordship over them; and their great ones exercise authority upon them.
>
> But so shall it not be among you: but whosoever will be great among you, shall be your minister:
>
> And whosoever of you will be the chiefest, shall be servant of all.
>
> For even the Son of man came not to be ministered unto, but to minister, and to give his life a ransom for many. (Mark 10:42–45)

The Lord's priesthood holders are servants. Even those remarkable sibling Apostles needed to learn the principles governing the use of the priesthood. Priesthood is given to help men be better servants. That is the great lesson that each priesthood holder must learn.

The natural man often exercises unrighteous dominion over others. But priesthood holders in the Lord's kingdom must learn that their calling is to serve. Jesus exemplified this lesson as He humbly served.

Priesthood holders learn to use their priesthood through experience. Then, when asked questions, they often share the experience that prompted the learning. This is characteristic of President

Thomas S. Monson's approach throughout his apostolic ministry. Over the years, President Monson has shared multiple experiences of how he learned his priesthood duty by ministering to others, rescuing the lost, and loving the wandering and wounded sheep in his flock. Priesthood principles and practice are learned as a priesthood holder serves others.

I have learned the application of many priesthood principles over the years. Following any priesthood service, the key for me is to ask, "How could I have done better?" I learned to ask this question from an experienced priesthood holder. On one occasion when I was an Area Seventy, I was assigned to accompany Elder Neal A. Maxwell of the Quorum of the Twelve to a stake conference. It was marvelous to be with one of the most remarkable gospel teachers of this dispensation. At the conference, I gained an insight into how he had developed and magnified what was undoubtedly a God-given gift. As we were driving away from the stake center on Saturday evening, he turned in his seat and asked me, "What could I have done better to teach the principles we taught?" I thought he had to be joking. But he kept on grilling me until I mentioned some minor thing that might have been slightly unclear. The next day, in the Sunday general session of the stake conference, he clarified that minor thing I had mentioned. I realized that I was with a humble Apostle of Jesus Christ who welcomed counsel and always desired to be a more effective priesthood holder.

A priesthood holder must continually be open to learning and applying priesthood principles by asking himself, "How can I do better?" When he accepts that priesthood principles are learned line upon line and precept on precept, he will be a better servant of the Lord.

Chapter 11

PRINCIPLE #3

A CALLING IN THE PRIESTHOOD
IS A CALLING TO SERVE

For I have given you an example,
that ye should do as I have done to you.

—JOHN 13:15

The doctrine of the priesthood inspires a priesthood holder to bless others. He is called to serve and minister. At the Last Supper, the Savior taught this principle to His Apostles. Knowing He would soon be taken, tried, and slain, Jesus washed the Apostles' feet. John records:

> He riseth from supper, and laid aside his garments; and took a towel, and girded himself.
>
> After that he poureth water into a basin, and began to wash the disciples' feet, and to wipe them with the towel wherewith he was girded. . . .
>
> So after he had washed their feet, and had taken his garments, and was set down again, he said unto them, Know ye what I have done to you?
>
> Ye call me Master and Lord: and ye say well; for so I am.

If I then, your Lord and Master, have washed your feet; ye also ought to wash one another's feet.

For I have given you an example, that ye should do as I have done to you.

Verily, verily, I say unto you, The servant is not greater than his lord; neither he that is sent greater than he that sent him.

If ye know these things, happy are ye if ye do them. (John 13:4–5, 12–17)

The Lord taught by both His words and His actions. His instruction was clear. The Apostles were to follow His example by serving others. The Lord promised them happiness if they followed His example.

Happiness for a priesthood holder comes by exercising his priesthood by serving others. He cannot be happy by being idle. Happiness for a priesthood holder is eternally linked with service.

President Marion G. Romney taught: "Service is not something we endure on this earth so that we can earn the right to live in the celestial kingdom. Service is the very fiber of which an exalted life in the celestial kingdom is made."[1] For a priesthood holder, service is eternally intrinsic to his calling and to his eternal happiness. All priesthood holders, including leaders, have service as their focus.

In the corporate world, service is the job of the underlings. This is manifest in the typical organizational chart for most companies. If priesthood were organized like a company, the organizational chart would look like Figure 3 on page 98, suggesting that a stake president is served by other administrative leaders, individuals, and families.

Now let us consider the organizational chart for the Lord's Church that is suggested by Paul in his letter to the Ephesians.

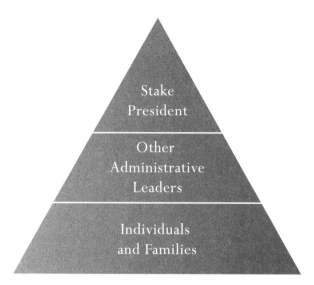

Figure 3: The World's Way.

Now therefore ye are no more strangers and foreigners, but fellowcitizens with the saints, and of the household of God;

And are *built upon the foundation* of the apostles and prophets, Jesus Christ himself being the chief corner stone;

In whom all the building fitly framed together groweth unto an holy temple in the Lord:

In whom ye also are built together for an habitation of God through the Spirit. (Ephesians 2:19–22; emphasis added)

In this structure, the leaders—Jesus Christ and the Apostles— are at the bottom of the pyramid so that they can serve individuals and families. They also provide the foundation that supports the rest of the structure. If we draw an organizational chart following this pattern, the structure looks like Figure 4 on page 99.

The pattern of a servant-leader is found through the Lord's Church. The priesthood leader is the servant of all, following the pattern set by Jesus Christ. It is obvious that the Lord's Church and

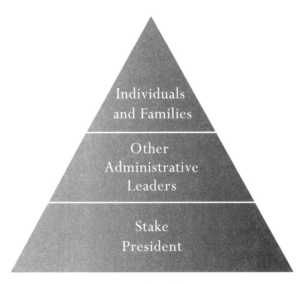

Figure 4: The Lord's Way.

priesthood are set up to work differently than typical organizations in the world.

A corollary priesthood principle is found at other times in the Lord's ministry. The minister focuses on people and not on efficiency. On one occasion recorded in the New Testament, parents sought blessings for their children. The disciples "rebuked" these parents. The Joseph Smith Translation of Matthew 19 helps us understand that the disciples knew that children did not need such blessings for their salvation. These disciples believed that blessing these children posed an unnecessary burden on the Savior.

> Then were there brought unto him little children, that he should put his hands on them, and pray. And the disciples rebuked them, saying, There is no need, for Jesus hath said, Such shall be saved.
>
> But Jesus said, Suffer [or permit] little children, and forbid them not, to come unto me: for of such is the kingdom of heaven.

And he laid his hands on them, and departed thence. (JST, Matthew 19:13–15)

The Savior ministered; He blessed. Certainly, He knew that the blessings He provided were not necessary for the children's salvation, so why did He bless the children? He knew that such a blessing would bring comfort and peace to the parents and to the children. Was it more work for Him? Yes! Did He provide the blessings to help others? Yes! When it comes to exercising priesthood, is it more important to minister than to be efficient? Yes!

After Jesus' death and resurrection, we find an instructive event that took place in the Americas. The resurrected Savior appeared and taught the people. He perceived that they did not completely understand His teachings and asked them to go to their homes and ponder the things they had heard. He did, after all, have other, non-trivial work to do. He needed to go to Heavenly Father and to the lost tribes of Israel. Yet, He postponed the important work to minister to the people (see 3 Nephi 17:2–4).

"And it came to pass that when Jesus had thus spoken, he cast his eyes round about again on the multitude, and beheld they were in tears, and did look steadfastly upon him as if they would ask him to tarry a little longer with them.

"And he said unto them: Behold, my bowels are filled with compassion towards you" (3 Nephi 17:5–6).

Remarkably, the Savior did not go on His appointed errands, despite their importance. He sensed a longing for His continued presence that triggered a desire to help the multitudes. He offered a way to bless the people. He asked: "Have ye any that are sick among you? Bring them hither. Have ye any that are lame, or blind, or halt, or maimed, or leprous, or that are withered, or that are deaf, or that are afflicted in any manner? Bring them hither and I will heal them, for I have compassion upon you; my bowels are filled with mercy" (3 Nephi 17:7).

Then, motivated by His compassion toward them, He healed, blessed, and cured all their woes. "And it came to pass that when he had thus spoken, all the multitude, with one accord, did go forth with their sick and their afflicted, and their lame, and with their blind, and with their dumb, and with all them that were afflicted in any manner; and he did heal them every one as they were brought forth unto him" (3 Nephi 17:9).

Then, further ministering became a life-altering experience for the Nephite children. Jesus commanded that the children be brought to Him, and Jesus knelt and prayed to the Father.

> And it came to pass that when Jesus had made an end of praying unto the Father, he arose; but *so great was the joy of the multitude that they were overcome.*
>
> And it came to pass that Jesus spake unto them, and bade them arise.
>
> And they arose from the earth, and he said unto them: Blessed are ye because of your faith. And now behold, *my joy is full.*
>
> And when he had said these words, he wept, and the multitude bare record of it, and he took their little children, one by one, and blessed them, and prayed unto the Father for them. (3 Nephi 17:18–21; emphasis added)

The Savior's joy was full at least in part because of the great joy the multitude felt. But what of the other tasks the Savior still had left to do? He still accomplished them—but only after He served the people. The lesson for a priesthood holder is clear: Serving people takes priority over most everything else. True happiness comes through ministering and serving.

President Thomas S. Monson has said: "The priesthood is not

really so much a gift as it is a commission to serve, a privilege to lift, and an opportunity to bless the lives of others. A priesthood holder never lets efficiency get in the way of ministering to an individual. A program is not more important than a person."[2]

Often the opportunity to serve is not convenient. Heavenly Father's children do not schedule their emergencies. Just as the Savior postponed important business to minister to the multitude in the Americas, priesthood holders must often postpone other activities in order to serve. While serving as a bishop, I was also a busy physician. One night I had had no sleep because I had been in the hospital caring for sick patients. As I was returning home, I received a phone call from a distressed ward member. Her husband had been incarcerated and was scheduled for deportation from the United States the following morning. I remember being so tired, wishing I could get some rest before having to think of anything else.

Instead of going home, I drove to the jail. I prayed that the Lord would help me and the family. As I arrived at the jail, a thought came that I should contact an individual with whom I was acquainted. I did so, and she provided some additional contacts that led to the release of the ward member. A later judicial hearing eventually led to resolution of the immigration issue for this young family. I was grateful that I put my own convenience aside and served when the need arose.

Often, when I am assigned to attend conferences, mission tours, leadership meetings, or other functions, I feel that somewhere in the congregation is an individual whom I need to find and serve. Once, we arrived late one night in Saskatoon, Canada. The next day, we were participating in several meetings. We were very much looking forward to having a couple of hours in the morning to prepare further for the meetings. A stake president picked us up at the airport and drove us to a hotel. As he was dropping us off at midnight, he said, "I know I shouldn't ask you, but we have a member of our stake who is desperately ill, and I feel he and his family would be helped if you gave him a blessing."

Sister Renlund and I looked at each other and knew that there was only one way to respond. Earlier than we had planned, we arose the next morning and went with the stake president to minister to a family in need and a beloved son of Heavenly Father. It turned out to be the most meaningful part of our visit to Saskatoon.

NOTES

1. Marion G. Romney, in Conference Report, October 1982, 135.

2. Thomas S. Monson, "Do Your Duty—That Is Best," *Ensign,* November 2005.

Chapter 12

PRINCIPLE #4
A PRIESTHOOD HOLDER RECOGNIZES AND FOLLOWS RIGHTEOUS PATTERNS

And again, I will give unto you a pattern in
all things, that ye may not be deceived.
—DOCTRINE AND COVENANTS 52:14

The Lord has revealed patterns by which a priesthood holder may know that he and others with whom he interacts are acting under inspiration. A pattern of who is entitled to receive revelation and speak for God in the Church was revealed early in this dispensation (see Doctrine and Covenants 28:2, 7; see also chapter 3 of this book). That pattern helps priesthood holders avoid mistakes and deception.

Regardless of the motivation, it has always been tempting for members to give counsel and advice to leaders in the Church. Oliver Cowdery was warned that he should "not command him who is at [his] head, and at the head of the church" (Doctrine and Covenants 28:6). The Prophet Joseph Smith remarked on and further developed this pattern:

It is contrary to the economy of God for any member of the Church, or any one, to receive instructions for those in authority, higher than themselves; therefore you will see the impropriety of giving heed to them; but if any person have a vision or a visitation from a heavenly messenger, it must be for his own benefit and instruction; for the fundamental principles, government, and doctrine of the Church are vested in the keys of the kingdom.[1]

This pattern helped me deal with an uncomfortable situation. While I was serving as an Area Seventy in Utah, I received a phone call from a man from out of state. This man had called Church headquarters and, for unknowable reasons, the operator had transferred the call to me. The man explained, in all seriousness, that he had received a revelation that there was another ancient text buried in the basement of a home in Salt Lake City. This text would be of great benefit to the Church. The man had previously gone to the home, but as he did not own it, he was arrested by the police for trespassing. The man now wanted my help to get to the record. After listening to his plea for a long time, I simply said, "No."

The man continued to plead and eventually asked if I would at least pray about it. Again, I said, "No." The man was somewhat dumbfounded that I would not even consider praying about the matter. I then briefly explained the priesthood pattern of revelation and told him that he was in no position to receive revelation for the Church. A message for the whole Church comes through God's appointed servants.

A second important priesthood pattern helps us know whom to trust. Joseph Smith was admonished to be careful because he would not always know whom he could rely on. Joseph could not always discern the character and intent of another. He was told: "But as you cannot always judge the righteous, or as you cannot always tell the wicked from the righteous, therefore I say unto you, hold your peace until I shall see fit to make all things known unto the world concerning the matter" (Doctrine and Covenants 10:37).

The Lord gave him a valuable pattern to help him avoid deception.

> And again, I will give unto you *a pattern in all things,* that ye may not be deceived; for Satan is abroad in the land, and he goeth forth deceiving the nations—
>
> Wherefore he that prayeth, whose spirit is contrite, the same is accepted of me if he obey mine ordinances.
>
> He that speaketh, whose spirit is contrite, whose language is meek and edifieth, the same is of God if he obey mine ordinances.
>
> And again, he that trembleth under my power shall be made strong, and shall bring forth fruits of praise and wisdom, according to the revelations and truths which I have given you.
>
> And again, he that is overcome and bringeth not forth fruits, even according to this pattern, is not of me.
>
> Wherefore, *by this pattern* ye shall know the spirits in all cases under the whole heavens. (Doctrine and Covenants 52:14–18; emphasis added)

The Lord reveals a pattern that can be applied to "all cases." The first element of the pattern is that the person is obedient. He must comply with the ordinances of the gospel and do his best to be worthy. If an individual is not obedient, then what he advocates or advises is suspect.

The second element requires that the individual manifests a contrite spirit. This means there is no air of superiority, no "holier-than-thou" attitude. He is not self-righteous, self-aggrandizing, or self-promoting. He does not seek to dominate, demand, or debate.

The third element is that the individual's speech will be edifying.

His conversation will build others. It will be faith-promoting, not fear-inducing. It will never be crushingly brutal, demeaning, harsh, or derogatory.

The fourth element is that it will be manifest that the individual is influenced by the power of God. He will be willing to change his mind, as directed by the Spirit. He understands that revelation is precious. He will not "take up God's time" on trivial matters. As Joseph Smith said:

> We never inquire at the hand of God for special revelation only in case of there being no previous revelation to suit the case. . . . It is a great thing to inquire at the hands of God, or to come into His presence; and we feel fearful to approach Him on subjects that are of little or no consequence, to satisfy the queries of individuals, especially about things the knowledge of which men ought to obtain in all sincerity, before God, for themselves, in humility by the prayer of faith.[2]

The fifth element is that others listening to the individual are edified by his speech. Others will praise the speaker for his wisdom.

This pattern was not only helpful in Joseph's day, it is applicable in successful Church and family councils today. Using this pattern helps priesthood holders avoid deception and promotes reliable revelation.

The third pattern that may help a priesthood holder is recognizing that when God directs the work, the work is not frustrating. Consider this statement:

> The works, and the designs, and the purposes of God cannot be frustrated, neither can they come to naught.
>
> For God doth not walk in crooked paths, neither doth he turn to the right hand nor to the left, neither doth he vary

from that which he hath said, therefore his paths are straight, and his course is one eternal round.

Remember, remember that it is not the work of God that is frustrated, but the work of men. (Doctrine and Covenants 3:1–3)

When priesthood holders are feeling frustrated, they need to take time to examine their own actions and motivations. On one occasion, I was asked to help resolve an audit difficulty arising in a small branch. The branch clerk, an elderly, uneducated man, brought the reports and account ledgers to the meetinghouse. We began working through the calculations and could not get the accounts to balance. After hours of frustration, the elderly man said, "Brother Renlund, I think we should have started with prayer." I agreed. We knelt, and this man offered a sincere, pleading prayer. We then returned to the task and found the error immediately. Humbled, I learned that in all things, we need to ask the Lord for His help in His work. If we are frustrated, it is often because we are not doing things the Lord's way.

Other patterns are observed in the scriptures. The Savior provided a pattern for prayer (see Matthew 6:9–13). However, He did not intend that an identical prayer be the only one offered on every occasion. The pattern is what is important: address Heavenly Father, express gratitude, and request the needed help.

Some patterns are learned by observing the leaders of the Church. Elder Spencer W. Kimball said: "No one in this Church will ever go far astray who ties himself securely to the Church Authorities whom the Lord has placed in His Church. This Church will never go astray; the Quorum of the Twelve [and the First Presidency] will never lead into bypaths; it never has and never will."[3]

While priesthood holders should be quick to follow righteous patterns, they must be careful not to create unintended patterns.

For instance, always having a married couple say the invocation and benediction in a meeting could set an unintended expectation that only married people pray publicly.

I sent an unintended message in a surprising way while serving as a bishop. One day at Church, a new convert approached Sister Renlund and asked if she could ask a serious, important question. Sister Renlund said, "Of course." This woman then asked, "What is the significance of the bishop's red tie?" The significance was that I owned one nice tie and it was red; I wore it to Church every Sunday. We might smile, but we should remember that even something as simple as the pattern of wearing a red tie can be mistaken as having some deeper meaning.

Patterns offer a way by which a priesthood holder knows whom to trust and whom to follow. Patterns are found in the scriptures and in the operations of the Church. Priesthood holders must carefully follow God's patterns and avoid setting unintended ones.

NOTES

1. Joseph Smith, *Teachings of Presidents of the Church: Joseph Smith* (2007), 197–98.

2. Joseph Smith, *Teachings of the Prophet Joseph Smith,* comp. Joseph Fielding Smith (1976), 22.

3. Spencer W. Kimball, in Conference Report, April 1951, 104.

Chapter 13

PRINCIPLE #5

A PRIESTHOOD HOLDER'S IDENTITY
BECOMES CHRISTLIKE

I am made all things to all men,
that I might by all means save some.
—1 CORINTHIANS 9:22

Ministering—blessing, supporting, and loving—is at the heart of priesthood service. An effective priesthood holder becomes a disciple of Jesus Christ, in large part, to help others come unto Christ (see Moroni 7:48). Being a faithful disciple in order to help others become faithful disciples is the purpose behind every priesthood calling in the Church.[1]

Priesthood holders, however, may be unaware that their own attitudes and attributes may hinder their ministry. I learned this from an interaction we had with a friend in South Africa. My friend was a former stake president, mission president, and Regional Representative. He said, "We South Africans don't like to be told what to do by Americans." It caused me to ask why he would say this. At the time, I was serving as the Area President of the Africa Southeast Area of the Church. What did this statement say about how our friend saw me? How did his view of me affect my ability to effectively minister?

After consideration, I concluded that as a priesthood holder I had to do two things. First, I had to make a conscientious effort to view others without my prejudices and biases. Second, I had to help others minimize whatever prejudices and biases they might have related to me. Everyone naturally sees the world through his or her own filters or lenses. These filters may include nationality, race, traditions, profession, or culture. They express themselves as preferences for language, appearance, or habits.

Such filters may prevent a priesthood holder from seeing a person as he or she truly is—a son or daughter of God. The priesthood holder needs to plead with Heavenly Father to eliminate personal filters. His goal should be to see others as God sees them and minister to others as the Savior did. In doing so, he will subjugate his personal identity for the sake of claiming a higher identity, an identity as a disciple of Jesus Christ.

"If any man come to me, and hate [the Greek word translated as "hate," *miseo,* means to "love me more" or "put me first"] not his father, and mother, and wife, and children, and brethren, and sisters, yea, and his own life also, he cannot be my disciple" (Luke 14:26).

As the priesthood holder puts his discipleship before his own identity, he will see others more clearly and minister more effectively. Clearly seeing people as they really are has a profound impact.

My medical career focused on patients who were very ill, those with heart failure. One of the treatments for heart failure is a heart transplant. I cared for many patients who waited for and received new hearts. Over time, I saw too many individuals succumb to their illness. Sometimes I kept an emotional distance, a clinical objectivity, to avoid feeling overwrought each time a patient passed away.

I would tell myself that at least the patient received the best care that could have been given.

On one occasion, my clinical objectivity shattered. A young man, Chad, developed heart failure. At age eighteen, he underwent a heart transplant. He did well for many years and tried to live as normal a life as possible. Chad's efforts were heroic. He served a mission and contributed to the happiness and joy of his parents and other family members. Fifteen years after his transplant, Chad's health began to decline, and he was repeatedly hospitalized. One evening, Chad was brought to the emergency room in cardiac arrest. My medical team worked for a long time trying to save him, but the attempt failed. Eventually, I directed that the resuscitative efforts cease and declared Chad dead.

I felt sadness and disappointment but objectively thought, "Well, at least he had many good years." This emotional distance completely disappeared as Chad's parents were brought into the emergency room bay where Chad lay dead on a stretcher. In that moment, I saw Chad through the eyes of his loving parents. I saw the love, hope, and desires they had for him. I could not stop my tears as I sensed the great sadness Chad's parents felt.

Seeing Chad through his parents' eyes changed me. I have since had a heightened awareness of the need to see others here on earth as Heavenly Father sees them. A priesthood holder is forever changed if he too can see through heaven's eyes. Once a priesthood holder eliminates his natural biases and prejudices, he can help those he serves minimize their prejudices and biases toward him. When he is recognized as a disciple of Jesus Christ, it makes it possible for those he serves to look past the man.

The Apostle Paul described his own need to eliminate filters in order to be an effective priesthood holder:

> For though I be free from all men, yet have I made myself servant unto all, that I might gain the more.
>
> And unto the Jews I became as a Jew, that I might gain the Jews . . .
>
> To them that are without law, [I became] as without law . . . that I might gain them that are without law.
>
> To the weak became I as weak, that I might gain the weak: I am made all things to all men, that I might by all means save some.
>
> And this I do for the gospel's sake. (1 Corinthians 9:19–23)

Paul knew that to be effective as a priesthood holder, he needed to accentuate the characteristics that made him like those to whom he was called to minister. Paul wanted others to look past his outward characteristics and see a disciple of Jesus Christ. Similarly, priesthood holders must become genuine disciples of the Jesus Christ in order to effectively minister. They can do this only with the Lord's help, as He has said, "My grace is sufficient for the meek, that they shall take no advantage of your weakness" (Ether 12:26). Through His grace, the priesthood holder's outward characteristics diminish so that all others see is a disciple of the Savior.

A priesthood holder who is serious about incorporating the attributes of Jesus Christ into his character may find it helpful to consider the following:

- Though omniscient, Jesus Christ never acted like an insufferable know-it-all. How can a priesthood holder ensure that his education and knowledge are not barriers to others?
- Though omnipotent and having overcome all things, Jesus Christ was meek and humble. How can a priesthood holder ensure that he is meek and humble in the face of his own accomplishments?
- Though capable of the loftiest language, Jesus spoke in

simple terms, seeking to be understood by those He taught. How can a priesthood holder ensure that he speaks and teaches to the understanding of others?

NOTE

1. *Handbook 2: Administering the Church* (2010), section 3.1.

Chapter 14

Principle #6

Priesthood Power and Influence Are Maintained Using Christlike Attributes

. . . by persuasion, by long-suffering,
by gentleness and meekness, and by love . . .
—Doctrine and Covenants 121:41–42

The doctrine of the priesthood requires that priesthood authority be exercised in the same way Christ exercises His authority. The Lord emphatically states:

"No power or influence can or ought to be maintained by virtue of the priesthood, only by persuasion, by long-suffering, by gentleness and meekness, and by love unfeigned;

"By kindness, and pure knowledge, which shall greatly enlarge the soul without hypocrisy, and without guile" (Doctrine and Covenants 121:41–42).

Other powers or influences, such as force, guilt, or coercion in any degree, are not sanctioned. Using any other power or influence violates the doctrine of the priesthood. President Joseph F. Smith explained:

There is not a man holding any position of authority in the Church who can perform his duty as he should in any other spirit than in the spirit of fatherhood and brotherhood toward those over whom he presides . . . [they] . . . should not be rulers, nor dictators; they should not be arbitrary; they should gain the hearts, the confidence and love of those over whom they preside, by kindness and love unfeigned, by gentleness of spirit, by persuasion, by an example that is above reproach.[1]

Agency, the eternal principle of progression, is a God-given ability to act and not to be acted upon. A priesthood holder exercises influence only when another allows him to. For example, every person in a ward "presides" over the bishop, in a sense, by retreating across his threshold and saying, "No." A priesthood holder may influence by persuading, encouraging, coaxing, and urging. When that is coupled with long-suffering, forgiveness, tolerance, accommodation, and patience, the priesthood holder acts in a Christlike manner. An effective priesthood holder exhibits mildness, calmness, tenderness, and even submissiveness. He loves sincerely and genuinely and respects the individual's agency. A righteous priesthood holder is not pushy and aggressive; rather, he shows compassion, sympathy, thoughtfulness, and consideration.

Christlike attributes must be cultivated. The priesthood holder uses "pure knowledge that will greatly enlarge the soul" in influencing others. This means that he uses gospel knowledge, not rhetorical techniques or tricks, in persuading others. He does not resort to duplicity, shading of truth, wiliness, craftiness, cleverness, or deceit. He is always honest.

Peter wrote that for priesthood holders to be effective and receive the great and precious promises of the Savior, they need to take on themselves divine attributes.

Whereby are given unto us exceeding great and precious promises: that by these ye might be partakers of the divine nature, having escaped the corruption that is in the world through lust.

And beside this, giving all diligence, add to your faith virtue; and to virtue knowledge;

And to knowledge temperance; and to temperance patience; and to patience godliness;

And to godliness brotherly kindness; and to brotherly kindness charity.

For if these things be in you, and abound, they make you that ye shall neither be barren nor unfruitful in the knowledge of our Lord Jesus Christ. (2 Peter 1:4–8)

A priesthood holder must develop a divine nature; he must become virtuous, temperate, patient, godly, kind, and charitable so that he may effectively invite all to come unto Christ. This may sound like an impossible task, but by daily practice and focus, we can all progress.

President Thomas S. Monson has over a lifetime inculcated into his very being Christlike attributes. Many have observed his kindness from afar. We saw it up close. When I was called as a General Authority in 2009, I was set apart by President Monson. He took the time to teach, sharing some of his experiences, illustrating principles that he thought would be helpful for me. After I was set apart, President Monson gave Ruth a big hug and asked her to share his love with the Saints wherever we encountered them.

We felt blessed for the time President Monson had taken with us. I remarked, "President Monson, you have been unbelievably generous and gracious with the time you have spent with us." Somewhat surprised, President Monson said, "I have only treated you as I would like to be treated." This small interaction allowed us to see that President Monson lives this teaching from the Savior:

"And as ye would that men should do to you, do ye also to them likewise" (Luke 6:31).

President Monson's example has been an inspiration to us. Treating others as we would like to be treated is a core aspect of priesthood service. Priesthood holders minister most effectively when they minister using Christlike attributes. These attributes allow priesthood influence to bless people in meaningful and lasting ways.

NOTE

1. Joseph F. Smith, in Conference Report, October 1904, 5.

Chapter 15

PRINCIPLE #7
A PRIESTHOOD HOLDER MUST BE WILLING TO BE PRESIDED OVER

Obey them that have the rule over you.

—HEBREWS 13:17

Priesthood holders may be called to preside in quorums, wards, and stakes. Whether they are called to preside or not, they face a test of leadership and ability. President Joseph F. Smith described the test as follows: "Every man should be willing to be presided over; and he is not fit to preside over others until he can submit sufficiently to the presidency of his brethren."[1]

In other words, we demonstrate leadership and ability by submitting to the presiding authority of another.

Before becoming a leader in the Lord's kingdom, a priesthood holder must be willing to be presided over. This principle applies to a deacons quorum president, who must submit sufficiently to the bishop's presiding authority. It applies to bishops, who must submit sufficiently to the presiding authority of the stake presidency. It applies to stake presidencies, who must submit sufficiently to the Seventy, the Twelve, and the First Presidency. It applies to the Seventy, who must submit sufficiently to the direction of the Twelve. It applies to members of the Quorum of the Twelve, who must submit sufficiently to the First Presidency. It applies to the President of the Church, who must submit sufficiently to the presiding authority of the Savior. Interestingly, this principle also applies to the Savior, who repeatedly demonstrated His submission to the will of the Father. In short, this principle applies to all priesthood holders.

When I was called as a stake president, I was thirty-nine years old and nervous. I was inexperienced and not well known among the stake leaders and stake members. Many were more qualified than I and, in my opinion, would have been a better choice. Although I sensed that my call was from God, I still felt insecure.

After I had been sustained, the stake patriarch, an experienced priesthood leader, approached me. The patriarch had previously served as a bishop, stake president, and Regional Representative. With a friendly smile and a warm handshake, he said simply, "I welcome your supervision of my calling." This statement of support and acceptance of my call reassured me and let me know that this man understood the doctrine of the priesthood. He was willing to be presided over by someone duly called and sustained.

This principle of the doctrine of the priesthood—following those who are called to lead—is demonstrated in a story from the life of Karl G. Maeser, an educator and leader in Church education. According to his biographer:

> His ability to teach lessons by simple examples is illustrated in an incident which happened while he and a party of missionaries were crossing the Alps. There were only sticks to mark the path across these mountains of deep snow. As they slowly ascended a steep slope, he looked back, saw this row of sticks marking the way and said, "Brethren, there stands the

Priesthood. They are just common sticks like the rest of us—some of them are even crooked, but the position they hold makes them what they are to us. If we step aside from the path they mark, we are lost."[2]

Although a priesthood holder must submit sufficiently to the presidency of those who preside over him, we do not believe that presiding brethren are infallible. The Lord works only with imperfect men who try their best. President Henry B. Eyring's father, a noted scientist, said:

> I am glad when one of the brethren says something that I think is a little bit foolish, because I think if the Lord can stand him, maybe he can stand me. So that's it, and I think that maybe there's a certain stumbling block that some of us have: we expect other people to be a kind of perfection that we don't even attempt to approach ourselves. We expect the brethren or the bishop or the stake president or the General Authorities to be not human, even. We expect the Lord to just open and shut their mouths, but He doesn't do that—they are human beings; but they're wonderful, and they do better than they would if it weren't for the Lord helping them.[3]

Some focus on a priesthood leader's imperfections as an excuse to reject that leader's presiding authority. Others recognize that the Lord uses imperfect men to accomplish His work. Priesthood holders do not have to be perfect to serve, only willing. As Elder Jeffrey R. Holland has said, "Except in the case of His only perfect Begotten Son, imperfect people are all God has ever had to work with. That must be terribly frustrating to Him, but He deals with it. So should we."[4]

Church history provides examples of priesthood holders who submitted sufficiently to presiding authority—and of others who did not. Those who pass the test of leadership and ability continue to uphold those who preside by their confidence, faith, and prayers. No one could have been a stauncher supporter of Joseph Smith than Brigham Young. His willingness to be presided over by Joseph is evident. During the difficult Kirtland period in Church history, many members were deserting the Church and Joseph Smith. Brigham Young said:

> It gave me sorrow of heart, and I clearly saw and understood, by the spirit of revelation manifested to me, that if I was to harbor a thought in my heart that Joseph could be wrong in anything, I would begin to lose confidence in him, and that feeling would grow . . . until at last I would have the same lack of confidence [as the apostates] in his being the mouthpiece of the Almighty. . . .
>
> Though I admitted in my feelings and knew all the time that Joseph was a human being and subject to err, still it was none of my business to look after his faults. . . . It was not for me to question whether Joseph was dictated by the Lord at all times and circumstances or not. . . . He was called of God . . . and if He [God] had a mind to leave him to himself and let him commit an error that was no business of mine. [Joseph Smith] was God's servant, and not mine.[5]

Brigham Young recognized that Church President's faults could be an impediment to some. It was not to him. He saw a bigger picture: "I never preached to the world but what the cry was, 'That damned old Joe Smith has done thus and so.' I would tell the people that they did not know him, and I did, and that I knew him to be a good man; and that when they spoke against him, they spoke against as good a man as ever lived."[6]

Brigham Young chose to be presided over by Joseph Smith, to defend and sustain him. That choice made all the difference both for Brigham Young and for the Church. Joseph Smith said, "Of the Twelve Apostles chosen in Kirtland . . . there have been but two but what have lifted their heel against me—namely Brigham Young and Heber C. Kimball."[7] Priesthood holders today have the same choice to make. They can choose to sustain Church leaders with their confidence, faith, and prayers and be like Brigham and Heber, or they can criticize their way right out of the Church (see Doctrine and Covenants 107:22).

Sufficiently submitting to the presidency of priesthood leaders means honoring the position and prerogatives of those who preside. In the biography of President Harold B. Lee, we read how he learned this lesson.

In 1922, Elder Harold B. Lee was a missionary serving as the conference president in Denver. On Saturday, February 18, Elder Lee was conducting a baptismal service when Elder James E. Talmage of the Twelve walked into the service. Elder Lee went forward with the service without consulting Elder Talmage. During the baptism, Elder Talmage stepped forward to the edge of the font and carefully watched what went on. When the confirmations started, the Apostle again stepped forward, uninvited, and said, "Here, I will confirm this one." After the service, when they were alone, Elder Talmage said, "Elder Lee, you did a splendid job, but . . ." and then proceeded to point out his error in not recognizing the presiding authority and in not checking with him before he proceeded.[8]

Honoring the position and prerogatives of the one who presides demonstrates submission to his presidency. This is the order of the priesthood.

How a priesthood holder responds to decisions made by those who preside over him is his choice, a choice with consequences. A tragic example was related by Elder George A. Smith on April 6, 1856:

While the Saints were living in Far West, there were two sisters wishing to make cheese, and, neither of them possessing the requisite number of cows, they agreed to exchange milk. The wife of Thomas B. Marsh, who was then president of the Twelve Apostles, and Sister Harris concluded they would exchange milk, in order to make a littler larger cheese than they otherwise could. To be sure to have justice done, it was agreed that they should not save the strippings [the cream that comes on the top of the milk], but that the milk and strippings should all go together. . . . Mrs. Harris, it appeared, was faithful to the agreement and carried to Mrs. Marsh the milk and strippings, but Mrs. Marsh, wishing to make some extra good cheese, saved a part of strippings from each cow and sent Mrs. Harris the milk without the strippings. Finally it leaked out that Mrs. Marsh had saved strippings, and it became a matter to be settled by the Teachers. They began to examine the matter, and it was proved that Mrs. Marsh had saved the strippings, and consequently had wronged Mrs. Harris out of that amount. An appeal was taken from the Teacher to the Bishop, and a regular Church trial was had. President Marsh did not consider that the Bishop had done him and his lady justice, for they decided that the strippings were wrongfully saved, and the woman had violated her covenant.

Marsh immediately took an appeal to the High Council, who investigated the question with much patience, and I assure you they were a grave body. Marsh being extremely anxious to maintain the character of his wife, as he was the President of the Twelve Apostles, and a great man in Israel, made a desperate defense, but the High Council finally confirmed the Bishop's decision.

Marsh, not being satisfied, took an appeal to the First Presidency of the Church, and Joseph and his Counselors had to sit upon the case, and they approved the decision of the

High Council. . . . Thomas B. Marsh then declared that he would sustain the character of his wife, even if he had to go to hell for it. The then President of the Twelve Apostles . . . went before a magistrate and swore that the Mormons were hostile towards the State of Missouri.[9]

"That affidavit resulted in an extermination order . . . written by Governor Boggs, the governor of Missouri."[10] On March 17, 1839, Elder Thomas B. Marsh was excommunicated.[11] Marsh's choice to defy presiding authorities is heartbreaking. A trifling disagreement and an unwillingness to submit sufficiently to the presidency of others affected him, his family, and the Church.

We are always blessed when we support priesthood leaders even if we feel aggrieved or disagree with a decision. A priesthood holder who passes the test of leadership and ability avoids the temptation to criticize, undermine, and dispute a presiding authority's decision. The Lord's priesthood order requires it.

NOTES

1. *Gospel Doctrine: Compiled Sermons of Joseph F. Smith* (1928), 206; John A. Widtsoe, *Priesthood and Church Government* (1962), 68.

2. Alma P. Burton, *Karl G. Maeser: Mormon Educator* (1953), 25–26.

3. Robert I. Eaton and Henry J. Eyring, *I Will Lead You Along: The Life of Henry B. Eyring* (2013), 29.

4. Jeffrey R. Holland, "Lord, I Believe," *Ensign,* May 2013.

5. Leonard J. Arrington, *Brigham Young: American Moses* (1985), 59–60.

6. Brigham Young, in *Journal of Discourses,* 26 vols. (1854–86), 4:77.

7. Joseph Smith, *Teachings of the Prophet Joseph Smith,* comp. Joseph Fielding Smith (1976), 307.

8. Francis M. Gibbons, *Harold B. Lee: Man of Vision, Prophet of God* (1993), 63.

9. George A. Smith, in *Journal of Discourses,* 3:283–84; see also *History of the Church of Jesus Christ of Latter-day Saints,* 7 vols. (1932–51), 3:167.

10. *History of the Church,* 3:173.

11. Ibid., 284.

Chapter 16

PRINCIPLE #8
A PRIESTHOOD HOLDER
SERVES WHERE CALLED

It shall not be given to any one . . . to build up my church,
except he be ordained by some one who has authority.

—DOCTRINE AND COVENANTS 42:11

In the world today, ambitious individuals seek for leadership positions in order to control and govern others. They network, campaign, and forge alliances in the hope of advancing careers, earning money, or increasing social status. This style of leadership is contrary to the doctrine of the priesthood. A priesthood holder serves where called. As Elder Dallin H. Oaks has said: "There is no 'up or down' in the service of the Lord. There is only 'forward or backward,' and that difference depends on how we accept and act upon our releases and callings."[1]

By design, in the Lord's Church, priesthood holders have callings for a season and then are released. Their release is not a statement about the quality of the work they have done. Releases and calls come by inspiration, on the Lord's timetable.

A priesthood leader serves at the Lord's pleasure with humility and willingness. A remarkable example of this principle comes from the life of President J. Reuben Clark Jr., a counselor to President David O. McKay. From October 1934 to April 1951, President Clark and President McKay served as counselors in the First Presidency, first to President Heber J. Grant and then to President George Albert Smith. Throughout this time, President Clark served as first counselor and President McKay served as second counselor.

In general conference on April 9, 1951, five days after President Smith died, President McKay was sustained as President of the Church. President Stephen L Richards was sustained as first counselor in the First Presidency and President Clark as second counselor.

President Clark had for such a long time served as first counselor in the First Presidency, it seemed odd to many that he was now being asked to serve as second counselor. In his remarks after the change, he provided the principles underlying the Lord's pattern in the priesthood: "In the service of the Lord, it is not where you serve but how. In the Church of Jesus Christ of Latter-day Saints, one takes the place to which one is duly called, which place one neither seeks nor declines."[2]

Priesthood callings are not positions one seeks. Rather, they are callings from God. These callings are made known to the Church: "Again I say unto you, that it shall not be given to any one to go forth to preach my gospel, or to build up my church, except he be ordained by some one who has authority, and it is known to the church that he has authority and has been regularly ordained by the heads of the church" (Doctrine and Covenants 42:11).

A calling in the priesthood does not come to an individual because of anything he has done; a calling is not "earned." The Lord calls individuals for His purposes. When I was called to serve as a bishop, my older brother, Gary, called to congratulate me on my call. Gary said: "You shouldn't suppose that God has called you because of anything you have done. In fact, in your case, it is despite what you have done. God has called you for what He will accomplish through you." This is true for most priesthood holders.

Seeking the priesthood, or any position within the priesthood, for improper reasons brings God's condemnation. An instructive story is seen in the life of Korah in the Old Testament. Korah, a Levite, led 250 of Israel's most prominent leaders in demanding to receive more than the Levitical Priesthood. Korah sought the same priesthood that Moses held, the Melchizedek Priesthood, and accused Moses and Aaron of taking too much upon themselves (see Numbers 16:1–3).

Moses questioned why they wanted more authority than God had already given them, asking, "Seek ye the priesthood also?" (Numbers 16:8–10). The Lord commanded both Aaron, with the priesthood holders who followed him, and Korah, with those who followed him, to bring censers and incense to the tabernacle. Those claiming priesthood authority were asked to bring fire before the Lord as a symbol of their prayers and supplication.

> And it came to pass, as he had made an end of speaking all these words, that the ground clave asunder that was under them:
>
> And the earth opened her mouth, and swallowed them up, and their houses, and all the men that appertained unto Korah, and all their goods.
>
> They, and all that appertained to them, went down alive into the pit, and the earth closed upon them: and they perished from among the congregation. . . .
>
> And there came out a fire from the Lord, and consumed the two hundred and fifty men that offered incense. (Numbers 16:31–33, 35)

This dramatic end to those who sought priesthood power for themselves is a sobering lesson for all priesthood holders. When God calls, answer. When He does not call, hold your peace. Priesthood callings are not about God's love or approbation.

The First Presidency expressed this principle in 1914:

> Priesthood is not given for the honor or aggrandizement of man, but for the ministry of service among those for whom the bearers of that sacred commission are called to labor. Be it remembered that even our Lord and Master, after long fasting, when faint in body and physically weakened by exhausting vigils and continued abstinence, resisted the arch tempter's suggestion that he use the authority and power of his Messiahship to provide for his own immediate needs.[3]

Temptations to misuse the priesthood and seek priesthood advancement are not new. Power has the potential to corrupt men. Priesthood power must be used when and where the Lord directs.

Priesthood holders must also wait upon the Lord to call them; positions in the priesthood are not sought. Consequently, it is contrary to the doctrine of the priesthood to recommend oneself for a position. On occasion, individual priesthood holders may feel a spiritual impression that they will be called to a position. Sometimes, a person so inspired believes he has been informed by the Spirit that the calling will come to him. Thereafter he may be confused if the call does not come. A few explanations are possible. Rarely, the prompting was not from the Holy Ghost, rather an emotional response. Sometimes, the spiritual prompting, though real, is over-interpreted. The Spirit may be informing the priesthood holder that he is worthy, should the call be extended to him. In other words, he stands approved of the Lord. Even when another man is called, he can sense God's approbation for him.

A release from a priesthood calling is intrinsic to a call. A man serves diligently during the time that he holds the calling, but then graciously accepts the release. Priesthood holders will rarely feel adequately thanked for their service. When I was released as a stake president, I was expecting a big thank you from the presiding authorities. I had worked diligently for years and felt I deserved such thanks. The weekend came, and the presiding authorities were focused on the call of the new stake presidency. They were not focused on thanking the outgoing stake presidency. After the stake conference, I felt disappointed.

That Sunday afternoon, I visited my father. He was a man of few words. He listened as I grumbled about not being thanked. He said nothing. The next morning, however, the phone rang at 6:00 A.M. It was my dad. Without preamble, he said, "I've been thinking about what you were saying. I have one question for you: Who were you serving?" Then he hung up. In that moment, my dad taught me a valuable and enduring principle about priesthood service. We serve when called. We graciously accept releases. Our thanks comes from the Lord.

NOTES

1. Dallin H. Oaks, "The Keys and Authority of the Priesthood," *Ensign,* May 2014.

2. *Teachings of Presidents of the Church: David O. McKay* (2003), 38–48.

3. The First Presidency: Joseph F. Smith, Anthon H. Lund, and Charles W. Penrose, in *Improvement Era,* March 1914, 479.

Chapter 17

PRINCIPLE #9
A PRIESTHOOD HOLDER FULFILLS HIS DUTY

He that learns not his duty . . . shall
not be counted worthy to stand.

—DOCTRINE AND COVENANTS 107:100

Intrinsic to the doctrine of the priesthood is a requirement that a priesthood holder learn and fulfill his duty. The Lord Himself states: "Wherefore, now let every man learn his duty, and to act in the office in which he is appointed, in all diligence. He that is slothful shall not be counted worthy to stand, and he that learns not his duty and shows himself not approved shall not be counted worthy to stand" (Doctrine and Covenants 107:99–100).

President George Albert Smith added: "It is your duty first of all to learn what the Lord wants and then by the power and strength of His Holy Priesthood to magnify your calling in the presence of your fellows in such a way that the people will be glad to follow you."[1]

Learning his duty may be the easiest part of a priesthood holder's responsibility. Handbooks, training meetings, and scriptures all provide sources for learning our duty. Fulfilling that duty, however, is more difficult. President Thomas S. Monson admonished: "Brethren, it is in doing—not just dreaming—that lives are blessed. Others are guided, souls are saved. 'Be ye doers of the word, and not hearers only, deceiving your own selves' (James 1:22)."[2]

Why do some men fail to do their priesthood duty? Perhaps they feel that what they do is insignificant and they do not recognize how important their contributions are. Perhaps they lose interest for a time and cannot find any enthusiasm for serving others. Perhaps they become momentarily distracted, reasoning that surely a short "vacation" from duty will not be noticed.

An example from U.S. history may be helpful in illustrating how costly distraction can be in the performance of one's duty. In 1865, no specialized protection force guarded the U.S. president while he was in Washington, D.C. The Secret Service had yet to be institutionalized. The responsibility for guarding the president fell to the metropolitan police. On April 14, John F. Parker, a thirty-five-year-old police officer, was assigned to guard the president at Ford's Theater. His momentary distraction had momentous consequences for the country. Parker took a position at the rear of the theater box, close to an entrance leading into it. His orders were to stand there, fully armed, to permit no unauthorized person to pass into the box, and to protect the president at all hazards. From the spot where he was stationed, Parker could not see the stage or the actors, but he could hear the words the actors spoke. He became so interested in the play that he quietly deserted his post of duty and took a seat in the audience.

With Parker gone, an assassin, John Wilkes Booth, went to the door that led to the box. Through a little hole he had previously made, he saw the president seated in an upholstered rocking armchair. Booth opened the door, stepped into the box, raised his right hand, ran his eye along the barrel of a one-shot brass derringer pistol, targeted the head of his victim less than five feet away—and pulled the trigger. Lincoln died from the wound the next day.[3] Parker's momentary break from duty likely cost Abraham Lincoln his life. If Parker had stood guard as his duty demanded, the attack may have been deterred.

Similarly, priesthood holders cannot afford to miss a moment of performing their duty. The Lord has been direct: Those who shirk their duty "shall not be counted worthy to stand" (Doctrine and Covenants 107:100). A priesthood holder who conscientiously completes his assignment may never fully know what he has accomplished or prevented. He will, however, be able to say that he did his duty. Completing one's duty brings its own reward. Admiral Lord Horatio Nelson, a hero of the British Navy, orchestrated a major victory against the Spanish Armada. Nelson was mortally wounded during the battle. As he lay dying, he said at least three times, "Thank God I have done my duty."[4]

On one occasion, I attended a meeting with President James E. Faust and other stake presidents. Each was asked by President Faust how missionary work was going in his stake. Several indicated that they could be doing better. When I was asked, I told President Faust we had just called 100 stake missionaries and were seeing many baptisms in our Chinese branch and in our Lao-Thai branch. President Faust looked me in the eye and said, "So, you're pleased, are you?" I thought for a moment and responded, "Yes!" President Faust's eyes twinkled as he asked a follow-up question, "But, are you satisfied?" As I thought about saying that I was satisfied, I could tell it was the wrong answer and quickly said, "No." This brief exchange has caused me to reflect about fulfilling one's duty. If a priesthood holder has given his best effort, he can and should feel pleased with himself even if the outcome is disappointing. As missionaries are taught: "When you have done your very best, you may still experience disappointments, but you will not be disappointed in yourself. You can feel certain that the Lord is pleased."[5]

However, even if an outcome is spectacular, a priesthood holder cannot be completely satisfied. There is and will always remain more to do until "the purposes of God shall be accomplished, and the Great Jehovah shall say the work is done."[6]

When a priesthood holder fulfills his duty, he is blessed. The Prophet Joseph said, "If you do your duty, it will be just as well with you, as though all men embraced the Gospel."[7] When a priesthood holder fails to fulfill his duty, God holds him accountable. President John Taylor said, "If you do not magnify your callings, God will hold you responsible for those whom you might have saved had you done your duty."[8] President Thomas S. Monson loves this motto: "Do [your] duty, that is best; leave unto [the] Lord the rest!"[9]

NOTES

1. George Albert Smith, in Conference Report, April 1942, 14.

2. Thomas S. Monson, "Do Your Duty—That Is Best," *Ensign,* November 2005.

3. Carl Sandburg, *Abraham Lincoln: The Prairie Years and the War Years,* one volume ed. (2005), 708–9.

4. Christopher Hibbert, *Nelson: A Personal History* (1994).

5. *Preach My Gospel: A Guide to Missionary Service* (2004), 11.

6. Joseph Smith, "The Wentworth Letter"; see *History of the Church of Jesus Christ of Latter-day Saints,* 7 vols. (1932–51), 4:535–41. The Wentworth Letter was originally published in Nauvoo in the *Times and Seasons,* March 1, 1842.

7. Joseph Smith, *Teachings of the Prophet Joseph Smith,* comp. Joseph Fielding Smith (1976), 43.

8. *Teachings of Presidents of the Church: John Taylor* (2001), 164.

9. Thomas S. Monson, "Do Your Duty—That Is Best," *Ensign,* November 2005.

Chapter 18

PRINCIPLE #10
A PRIESTHOOD HOLDER DELEGATES AND ACCEPTS DELEGATED RESPONSIBILITY

This is the way that mine apostles,
in ancient days, built up my church unto me.
—DOCTRINE AND COVENANTS 84:106, 108

The work of the priesthood can rarely be done alone. Each priesthood holder needs help to accomplish all that God expects him to do. The book of Exodus teaches that Moses needed help in doing his duty. Israel fought against the armies of Amalek, with Joshua leading Israel's army. Moses went with Aaron and Hur to the top of a hill to oversee the battle. As Moses watched, he held up his hands. Israel prevailed. When he let down his hands, Amalek prevailed.

Moses grew weary as he had to continuously hold up his hands. "But Moses' hands were heavy; and they took a stone, and put it under him, and he sat thereon; and Aaron and Hur stayed up his hands, the one on the one side, and the other on the other side; and his hands were steady until the going down of the sun" (Exodus 17:12).

Moses learned that holding up his hands was necessary for his army to win. He likely did not know why that was true, but he knew that he could not hold up his hands alone. He needed Aaron and Hur to help him.

Later, Moses learned that he needed help in places other than just the battlefield. Moses was judging all matters that the people brought before him. He received advice from his father-in-law, Jethro, that carrying this burden alone was not sustainable.

> And Moses' father in law said unto him, The thing that thou doest is not good.
>
> Thou wilt surely wear away, both thou, and this people that is with thee: for this thing is too heavy for thee; thou art not able to perform it thyself alone.
>
> Hearken now unto my voice, I will give thee counsel, and God shall be with thee. . . .
>
> Teach them ordinances and laws. . . .
>
> Provide out of all the people able men . . . to be rulers of thousands, and rulers of hundreds, rulers of fifties, and rulers of tens:
>
> And let them judge the people . . . every great matter they shall bring unto thee, but every small matter they shall judge: so shall it be easier for thyself, and they shall bear the burden with thee. . . .
>
> Then thou shalt be able to endure. (Exodus 18:17–23)

Moses accepted Jethro's twofold advice: to teach correct principles and let the people govern themselves, and to delegate responsibilities to others who had been trained. Later, the Lord provided seventy of the elders of Israel to help Moses with his burden (see Numbers 11). As Moses delegated responsibility, Israel was blessed, and Moses did not wear himself out. He led Israel with vigor and energy until he was succeeded by Joshua (see Deuteronomy 34:7).

From Moses, a priesthood holder learns these three lessons: (1) God's work goes forward when a priesthood holder involves others; (2) One person cannot carry the work alone; and (3) Sharing burdens allows a man to endure to the end. Delegating and accepting responsibility are essential to accomplishing the Lord's work.

The Savior followed this pattern as well. He delegated responsibility when he commissioned twelve Apostles. Recognizing that more help was needed to carry on the work of salvation, He also commissioned the Seventy (see Luke 10:2). Other callings were added to His Church as the need arose (see Ephesians 4:11–13). The Apostles, Seventy, and those in other callings accepted the delegated responsibility to carry out the Lord's mission. In ancient days, the Church was built up by priesthood leaders delegating and priesthood holders accepting responsibilities.

Delegation serves multiple purposes. Not only does it help a priesthood holder with his burden, it strengthens and establishes the Church.

> And if any man among you be strong in the Spirit, let him take with him him that is weak, that he may be edified in all meekness, that he may become strong also.
>
> Therefore, take with you those who are ordained unto the lesser priesthood, and send them before you to make appointments, and to prepare the way, and to fill appointments that you yourselves are not able to fill.
>
> Behold, *this* is the way that mine apostles, in ancient days, built up my church unto me. (Doctrine and Covenants 84:106–108; emphasis added)

In the Lord's Church today, experienced priesthood holders work with those with less experience. I had a wonderful service opportunity that demonstrated why the Lord uses this pattern to establish the Church. In a remote town, I asked a branch president—a relatively new convert and recently ordained elder—if he wanted to visit families in his branch one Saturday morning. The two of us ventured out. The first man we visited, Brother Thomas, was dying of AIDS. After offering comfort and support, I asked if there was anything we could do for him. Brother Thomas asked for a blessing. The branch president was asked to anoint and I was asked to seal the anointing. It was apparent that the branch president had never participated in blessing the sick. He held the plastic container of consecrated oil about ten inches over Brother Thomas's head and squeezed out a very large drop that splattered on impact. The branch president then put his hands on Brother Thomas's head and said, "I put oil on your head to heal you. Amen." An experienced holder recognizes that this is not the prescribed language used in anointing the sick.

In this circumstance, I felt assured that God would not withhold a blessing from Brother Thomas simply because the anointing was not performed using the correct words. Recognizing that the branch president had done his best, I did not correct him in front of Brother Thomas. Rather, I put my hands on Brother Thomas's head, asked the branch president to put his hands on mine, and sealed the anointing in the usual fashion. Brother Thomas seemed pleased. Good-byes were offered, and the branch president and I left.

As we walked away, I put my arm around the branch president and said, "You have such great faith. You brought a wonderful spirit to that blessing. I am sure the Lord is pleased." I pulled out a copy of the white missionary handbook, gave it to the branch president, and asked him to read the instructions on administering to the sick. As the branch president read, he said, "Oh, no! I did it wrong." I repeated, "You had such great faith and brought a wonderful spirit. I am sure the Lord is pleased."

As we arrived at our next visit, I asked the branch president if he thought another blessing would be requested. The branch president said he thought so. I suggested that we review the missionary handbook before we entered the yard. A blessing was requested. The branch president performed the anointing, and I sealed the anointing. As we were leaving, I said, "President, you have such wonderful faith and brought such a wonderful spirit. Should we see how we did?" The branch president again reviewed the missionary handbook. As he did, he was sad to recognize that he had left out a prescribed element. I said, "Yes, but you brought such great faith and a wonderful spirit to the blessing. I am sure the Lord is pleased."

The branch president and I visited nine homes that day and gave priesthood blessings in six. The branch president performed the third anointing perfectly. With the sixth blessing, he sealed the anointing perfectly. As I left that remote town, I left a branch president who had "become strong" and who could, as he accompanied less experienced priesthood holders on the Lord's errand, build the Church as the Savior's Apostles had in ancient days.

Mentoring a less experienced priesthood holder may initially take more time and effort on the part of the more experienced priesthood holder. As the less experienced priesthood holder gains more experience, he performs better and better and eventually can perform as well as his mentor. The more experienced man must be patient and gentle when tasks are performed imperfectly. The Church grows as individuals grow. The Church does not grow by having the best "pray-er" pray. It grows by teaching someone who does not know how to pray, to pray. It is a responsibility of experienced priesthood holders to mentor less experienced ones.

Delegation shares the priesthood holder's burden, provides training to the less experienced person, and builds up and establishes the Church. Delegation also accelerates the work. Effectiveness is increased when two or more people work together. This is called synergy. The contribution of one individual can never have a value greater than 1. Three individuals working synergistically, however, can contribute a value greater than 3.

Figure 5.

An engineering example is illustrative. The vertical, bearing weight of a piece of wood that is 2" x 4" x 8' long is 945 pounds.

Two pieces of wood of that same size, bound together, can bear a load of 4,402 pounds. Three pieces bound together in unity can bear a load of 7,478 pounds. Thus, the weight-bearing load two pieces can handle is five times what one alone could handle and more than double what those pieces of wood could handle separately. Three together can handle eight times more weight than each piece of wood could handle separately, 1 + 1 + 1 = 8. This is synergy.

Priesthood holders work synergistically when they delegate effectively, involving others in the Lord's work. Delegation requires that priesthood holders are willing to accept delegated responsibility. Soon after I was called as a young bishop, I learned this principle the hard way. For a time during my medical training, I served as the bishop of a struggling, inner-city ward. The "labourers [were] few" (Matthew 9:37). One day, the phone rang and Sister Renlund answered. The caller relayed that a member of the ward was in the hospital, the same hospital where I worked, and desired a priesthood blessing. Sister Renlund called me at the hospital and reported the request. I said I was involved with a sick patient and could not get away. I asked Sister Renlund to call the elders quorum president and ask that he arrange for the blessing. Sister Renlund did just that. About an hour later, the phone rang again. Sister Renlund answered. The man on the other end said he had been asked by the elders quorum president to give a blessing to the member in need. But, he reasoned, since the bishop worked in the same hospital, it would be more convenient if the bishop would just provide the blessing.

The work of the priesthood goes forward only when priesthood holders are willing to accept delegated responsibility.

Countless examples of priesthood holders accepting delegated responsibilities are found in the scriptures. Joseph, who was sold into Egypt as a slave, accepted responsibility and performed well in Potiphar's household. Later, even though he was imprisoned, he accepted assignments from the prison warden.

> But the Lord was with Joseph, and shewed him mercy, and gave him favour in the sight of the keeper of the prison.
>
> And the keeper of the prison committed to Joseph's hand all the prisoners that were in the prison; and whatsoever they did there, he was the doer of it.
>
> *The keeper of the prison looked not to any thing that was under his hand;* because the Lord was with him, and that which he did, the Lord made it to prosper. (Genesis 39:21–23; emphasis added)

The impressive thing about Joseph is that he performed his assignments so that they prospered. A priesthood holder should make all his assignments prosper and thereby demonstrate his understanding of an important aspect of the doctrine of the priesthood.

Chapter 19

Principle #11

A Priesthood Holder Works Effectively in Councils

. . . that ye may know how to act and direct my church.

—Doctrine and Covenants 43:8–10

The doctrine of the priesthood facilitates the governing of the Church, which is performed in councils. "Under the keys of priesthood leadership at each level, leaders counsel together for the benefit of individuals and families. . . . Effective councils invite full expression from council members [both men and women] and unify their efforts in responding to individual, family, and organizational needs."[1]

Councils have been part of the work of salvation from the beginning of this dispensation. Properly functioning councils help leaders delegate. As Elder M. Russell Ballard taught, councils can "decrease the burden on all individual leaders and . . . extend the reach and impact of their ministry through the combined help of others."[2]

But not all councils in the Church are effective. Their effectiveness depends in large measure on how priesthood holders participate in and preside over councils. Councils have ancient roots. The Prophet Joseph Smith explained that councils were serious matters. He said:

> In ancient days councils were conducted with such strict propriety, that no one was allowed to whisper, be weary, leave the room, or get uneasy in the least. . . . It was understood in ancient days, that . . . if the president could spend his time, the members could also; but in our councils, generally, one will be uneasy, another asleep; one praying, another not; one's mind on the business of the council, and another thinking on something else.[3]

Perhaps the Prophet Joseph described a council that you participated in. A revelatory experience cannot be expected in a dysfunctional council. Joseph Smith also taught that in an effective council, members should take turns speaking, to make sure "that there may be perfect order in all things."[4] This echoes directions from the Lord: "Appoint among yourselves a teacher, and let not all be spokesmen at once; but let one speak at a time and let all listen unto his sayings, that when all have spoken that all may be edified of all, and that every man may have an equal privilege" (Doctrine and Covenants 88:122).

In many councils, priesthood holders and women come together to receive revelation. Once received, revelation clarifies the path forward. The Lord said: "Hearken, O ye elders of my church whom I have called, behold I give unto you a commandment, that ye shall assemble yourselves together to agree upon my word; . . . that ye may know how to govern my church and have all things right before me" (Doctrine and Covenants 41:2–3).

In addition to prompting revelation, counseling in councils facilitates instruction, edification, and making of commitments. The Lord says:

And now, behold, I give unto you a commandment, that when ye are assembled together ye shall instruct and edify each other, that ye may know how to act and direct my church, how to act upon the points of my law and commandments, which I have given.

And thus ye shall become instructed in the law of my church, and be sanctified by that which ye have received, and ye shall bind yourselves to act in all holiness before me—

That inasmuch as ye do this, glory shall be added to the kingdom which ye have received. Inasmuch as ye do it not, it shall be taken, even that which ye have received. (Doctrine and Covenants 43:8–10)

As priesthood holders and sister leaders strive to participate in successful councils, meetings that fully realize their potential, we should remember that the model for Church councils is not generally found in committee meetings in the world. Our council meetings should be patterned after the principles of leadership taught by the Savior.

Effective Church councils and committees stand in sharp contrast to those that function poorly. Optimally functioning Church councils and committees facilitate effective service of others, extend the reach of the leaders, and require the guidance of the Holy Spirit. Comparing the characteristics of a well-functioning council with a poorly functioning council may help members participate more effectively.

CHARACTERISTIC #1: *Goals*

Poorly functioning councils have limited, self-centered goals. Frequently, they deal with repetitive work or merely give the appearance of accomplishment. A council member may use his or her position to further an individual organization's agenda.

In contrast, effective Church councils strive to minister and to serve. Moroni's description of the Nephites during a period of righteousness encapsulates this aim: "And the church did meet together oft, to fast and to pray, and to speak one with another concerning the welfare of their souls" (Moroni 6:4).

In all well-functioning Church councils, the goals are always centered on the welfare of members' souls.

CHARACTERISTIC #2: *Roles of Council Members*

Members of dysfunctional councils come representing a constituency and may advocate an agenda, viewpoint, or program. Council meetings may be viewed as opportunities for a council member to manipulate the allocation of resources to benefit his or her constituency, asking, "How can others help my organization?"

Members of effective Church councils come representing available resources, usually those of an organization, like the Relief Society or the elders quorum. Keeping the purpose of the council meeting in mind, participants ask, "How can my organization help?" Meetings are viewed as opportunities to optimize use of resources and to increase the effectiveness of the council.

CHARACTERISTIC #3: *Preparation*

Members of ineffective councils rarely devote much time, thought, or energy to preparing for their meetings. Attendance at the meeting is usually considered sufficient.

Effective Church council members prepare for their meetings. They arrive ready to report on past assignments and on their progress since the last meeting; most of the work is accomplished between meetings. Council members prayerfully consider the topics under discussion, bring the Spirit, and are ready to listen for direction.

CHARACTERISTIC #4: *Agenda*

Inefficient councils frequently focus on calendaring and disseminating information, allowing those two tasks to consume most of the meeting. They use multi-item agendas, often dealing with each issue only superficially.

Effective Church councils calendar and disseminate information efficiently, using minimal meeting time. The emphasis of the meeting is problem solving through discussion, often focusing on a one-item agenda. Examples of useful questions or agenda items include:

1. How can we best help the Brown family?
2. How can we involve parents in the Young Men/Young Women activities and program?
3. How can we better prepare young men for missionary work?

The focus of the agenda and the question being posed dictate the success of the council. The Lord directs that councils should be focused. "Verily, verily, I say unto you, as I said unto my disciples, where two or three are gathered together in my name, *as touching one thing,* behold, there will I be in the midst of them—even so am I in the midst of you" (Doctrine and Covenants 6:32; emphasis added).

Usually, the fewer the items on the agenda, the better the focus.

CHARACTERISTIC #5: *Meeting Etiquette*

Poorly functioning councils tolerate tardiness; after all, council members are busy people! Council members allow other concerns to distract them from the business at hand, whether they daydream, have side conversations, or respond to text messages and phone calls. Council members may dismiss comments made by other members or denigrate contributions. Instead of solving problems, participants may try to avoid responsibility and blame.

Effective Church council members arrive on time, show respect for all participants, and are sensitive to the demands of time on others, particularly the presiding officer. They pay attention and actively participate in the discussion. They offer their perspective, advice, and inspiration. By focusing on helping others, council members strive to solve problems cheerfully.

CHARACTERISTIC #6: *Assignments*

Ineffective council members define a successful meeting as one in which they receive no new assignment. If they do get "stuck" with a project or assignment, they accept it grudgingly, sometimes with no intention of completing the task.

Effective Church council members accept delegated assignments willingly, possibly even volunteering to take on a project. They do everything possible to accomplish the task on time and actively look for ways to help priesthood leaders.

CHARACTERISTIC #7: *Statistics*

Participants in poorly functioning councils believe that generating statistics is a worthy goal, in and of itself. All statistics and reports are designed for someone else's benefit; the statistics are rarely used by the council itself.

Effective Church council members understand that statistics are most helpful at the ecclesiastical level at which they are generated. For example, a statistic reporting the percentage of children not attending Primary is much more helpful to a ward Primary president than to a stake president. Statistics are tools that can identify individuals who need attention, suggest areas of teaching emphasis, and indicate ways to improve effectiveness. Council members understand that a number in a report is really a member.

CHARACTERISTIC #8: *Decision Making*

Leaders of ineffective councils frequently announce decisions with little or no discussion, almost as benevolent decrees. Participants who hold minority opinions lobby for change. They may criticize the leader or undermine his leadership.

In effective Church councils, a leader conducts the discussion under the direction of the Spirit. Although he makes the final decision, he listens carefully to the opinions, advice, and concerns of the council members. He offers no opinion or decision until he has listened to all council members. Once a decision has been made, however, council members support the decision of the presiding authority as if it were their own.

CHARACTERISTIC #9: *Outcomes*

Some members of poorly functioning councils believe that a successful meeting must be scripted so that the minutes can be written before the meeting is held. Revelation is not anticipated or received.

The outcomes of effective Church councils are determined by revelation. Meetings are opened by prayer, inviting the Spirit to be present, and each participant prepares to listen for promptings. Participants leave the meeting feeling inspired and directed in their work.

When Church councils and committees function properly, they extend the reach of leaders, minister to the members, and assist the Lord in His work. As Elder M. Russell Ballard has said, "This is the miracle of church councils; listening to each other and listening to the Spirit! When we support one another in church councils, we begin to understand how God can take ordinary men and women and make them extraordinary leaders."[5]

Priesthood holders have the responsibility to participate in Church councils and make them effective. This includes helping other council members, both men and women, understand how to effectively participate. Leaders must do more listening than speaking to allow the Spirit to guide decision making. Elder Ballard has taught: "The day is long past when any one leader, either man or woman—or for that manner, any parent—can provide all that is desperately needed in the lives of our families and Church members. If we are to succeed in leading our Heavenly Father's children back home to Him, we must counsel together and help each other."[6]

NOTES

1. *Handbook 2: Administering the Church* (2010), section 4.1.

2. M. Russell Ballard, "Counseling with Our Councils," *Ensign,* May 1994.

3. Joseph Smith, *Teachings of the Prophet Joseph Smith,* comp. Joseph Fielding Smith (1976), 69.

4. Ibid., 93–94.

5. Ballard, "Counseling."

6. M. Russell Ballard, *Counseling with Our Councils: Learning to Minister Together in the Church and in the Family,* revised ed. (2012), x.

Chapter 20

PRINCIPLE #12
A PRIESTHOOD HOLDER SEES
HIMSELF AS EQUAL WITH OTHERS

The body hath need of every member . . .
that the system may be kept perfect.
—DOCTRINE AND COVENANTS 84:109–110

The doctrine of the priesthood prescribes that a priesthood holder is of no greater worth than anyone else. His position or priesthood does not qualify him for greater standing before God or among those to whom he ministers. This principle is described by Alma in the Church he established: "And the priest, not esteeming himself above his hearers, for the preacher was no better than the hearer, neither was the teacher any better than the learner; and thus they were all equal, and they did all labor, every man according to his strength" (Alma 1:26).

Those called as preachers and teachers did not consider themselves better than others. They were all equal. They all worked. They all contributed their energy and gifts. All were important to the Church.

The Lord made this point again in this dispensation: "Therefore,

150

let every man stand in his own office, and labor in his own calling; and let not the head say unto the feet it hath no need of the feet; for without the feet how shall the body be able to stand? Also the body hath need of every member, that all may be edified together, that the system may be kept perfect" (Doctrine and Covenants 84:109–10).

All are needed in the work of the Lord. In 1995, when President Gordon B. Hinckley was sustained as the President of the Church, he made a remarkable statement illustrating that every member is needed in the Church and is able to make a contribution equivalent to that of the Church's President. President Hinckley said:

> This church does not belong to its President. Its head is the Lord Jesus Christ, whose name each of us has taken upon ourselves. We are all in this great endeavor together. We are here to assist our Father in His work and His glory, "to bring to pass the immortality and eternal life of man" (Moses 1:39). Your obligation is as serious in your sphere of responsibility as is my obligation in my sphere. No calling in this church is small or of little consequence. All of us in the pursuit of our duty touch the lives of others. . . .
>
> You have as great an opportunity for satisfaction in the performance of your duty as I do in mine. The progress of this work will be determined by our joint efforts. Whatever your calling, it is as fraught with the same kind of opportunity to accomplish good as is mine. What is really important is that this is the work of the Master. Our work is to go about doing good as did He.[1]

All are needed and all are equal before God. A priesthood holder recognizes that because of the Atonement of Jesus Christ, all mankind may be redeemed. All receive the gift of God's grace. All receive a gift of agency, to act and "not to be acted upon" (2 Nephi 2:26). With this knowledge, a priesthood holder cannot impose his will on another. He treats all with dignity and respect. Doing otherwise is contrary to the doctrine of the priesthood.

Some years ago, a young man named Curtis was called to serve a mission. He was the kind of missionary every mission president prays for. He was focused and worked hard. At one point, he was assigned a missionary companion who was immature, socially awkward, and not particularly enthusiastic about getting the work done.

One day, while the elders were riding their bicycles, Curtis looked back and saw that his companion had inexplicably gotten off his bike and was walking. Silently, Curtis expressed his frustration to God; what a chore it was to be saddled with a companion he had to drag around to accomplish anything. Moments later, Curtis had a profound impression, as if God were saying to him, "You know, Curtis, compared to me, the two of you aren't all that different."

In a moment of inspiration, Curtis realized eternal truths: We are all equal before God, we are all important in His work, and we all make the contribution we can with the talents and abilities we have.

The doctrine of the priesthood respects that the talents and gifts of each person are valuable. A priesthood holder esteems others as himself and recognizes the innate value of others.

NOTE

1. Gordon B. Hinckley, "This Is the Work of the Master," *Ensign,* May 1995.

Chapter 21

Principle #13
A Priesthood Holder Works in Unity

*And while they were at variance one with
another they became very slothful.*

—DOCTRINE AND COVENANTS 101:50

The Lord has made it clear that unity is critical in the Church, including in the presiding councils. In the Quorums of the Twelve and the Seventy, the Lord directed: "And every decision made by either of these quorums must be by the unanimous voice of the same; that is, every member in each quorum must be agreed to its decisions, in order to make their decisions of the same power or validity one with the other" (Doctrine and Covenants 107:27).

The attributes and character traits that foster unity are elaborated: "The decisions of these quorums, or either of them, are to be made in all righteousness, in holiness, and lowliness of heart, meekness and long-suffering, and in faith, and virtue, and knowledge, temperance, patience, godliness, brotherly kindness and charity; because the promise is, if these things abound in them they shall not be unfruitful" (Doctrine and Covenants 107:30–31).

The exercise of Christlike attributes by priesthood holders fosters revelation. As God's will is revealed, unity develops.

Unity may not come easily, and it always comes at a cost. The cost is spending time together, discussing the issue until all are satisfied with the decision. The cost is submission of ego. The cost is a commitment to judge others and their ideas with best intent. The cost is sharing information so that all who participate understand an issue. This is particularly true in families. Priesthood holders must pay the price for unity to be achieved. The one who presides, whether in the Church or in the home, must feel the greater burden to achieve unity.

Unity in the family and in the Church comes when genuine trust is fostered and the priesthood holder sets aside his ego. He must recognize that priesthood activity is not about him or his ideas. It is always about others. This priesthood principle is illustrated in the life of Elder Neal A. Maxwell. When Elder Maxwell became a member of the Quorum of the Twelve:

> [He] consciously worked on himself to repress his former instincts to advocate particular interests or solutions, not wanting his hobbies or passions to seek undue attention in quorum discussions. He came to prize the collegial relationship of the Twelve, in which "one gets a chance to see if his ideas will have a life of their own." And if those ideas don't fly with the group, then "maybe you'd better let them go." After all, "if my views are sound, why is it that my Brethren don't see it that way?"[1]

Another important aspect of achieving unity depends on priesthood holders' willingness to share information with colleagues in the work. The Savior set the example. He called His disciples friends, fully informed colleagues who had willingly adopted His goals. The Savior said: "Henceforth I call you not servants; for the servant knoweth not what his lord doeth: but I have called you friends; for all things that I have heard of my Father I have made known unto you" (John 15:15).

By making known all things Heavenly Father made known to Him, Jesus provided vision for the work. Similarly, a priesthood holder shares information to create vision, set goals, and make plans. This priesthood pattern fosters real unity that brings the blessings of heaven. Withholding information under the belief that "information is power" creates distrust that destroys unity.

Not all information can be shared by a priesthood holder. In certain settings, he is required to keep confidences. This does not mean that he cannot share *some* information. A priesthood holder can share general information so all who are involved can maximize their efforts. For instance, a stake president may discuss circumstances with his counselors without disclosing identities. Using hypotheticals may also protect privacy while still allowing the leader to receive counsel. The stake president can also ask permission of an individual to discuss the situation with a counselor. A home teacher may be asked to keep confidences as well. He should honor such requests but can employ similar techniques to receive help from others.

Disunity does not bless the Lord's work. A cautionary tale is found in a parable regarding the redemption of Zion. A nobleman directed his servants to go to a choice piece of property and plant twelve olive trees. He instructed the servants to guard the olive trees, build a watchtower, and post watchmen to protect the fruit of the olive trees from enemies.

The servants followed almost all of the instructions. They planted the olive trees, built a hedge, and set watchmen to guard the trees (see Doctrine and Covenants 101:43–62). However, their unity in building the watchtower fractured. They began to reason among themselves.

What need hath my lord of this tower?

And consulted for a long time, saying among themselves: What need hath my lord of this tower, seeing this is a time of peace?

Might not this money be given to the exchangers? For there is no need of these things.

And while they were *at variance one with another* they became very slothful, and they hearkened not unto the commandments of their lord.

And the enemy came by night, and broke down the hedge; and the servants of the nobleman arose and were affrighted, and fled; and the enemy destroyed their works, and broke down the olive trees. (Doctrine and Covenants 101:47–51; emphasis added)

What allowed the destruction of all the servants' work? They were "at variance one with another." Some lost sight of the goal: to protect the fruit from enemies. They rationalized and justified themselves, despite having been warned. When disaster struck, the nobleman identified the servants' disobedience as the cause of the problem.

Disaster results today when the Lord's servants are not unified. Consider what happens in a ward if the leaders are not unified. Within a short time, the disunity inevitably infects the entire ward. The spirit of contention creeps in, and the Holy Spirit disappears. The previous good work of priesthood holders and auxiliary leaders vanishes. The Lord's work is stopped. Priesthood holders have a solemn obligation to ensure that they are not the cause of disunity.

In Africa, Sister Renlund and I accompanied a member of the Quorum of the Twelve and his wife to a stake conference. The stake president, thrilled to have an Apostle in attendance, suggested more than the usual number of musical numbers by the choir. The

Apostle meekly suggested that one of the numbers be eliminated. The stake president explained why he had made the recommendation. The Apostle again indicated his preference to eliminate the number. Again, the stake president insisted that the musical number be performed. It was clear that the Apostle presided. Yet, rather than introduce contention into the situation, he meekly said, "Okay."

This Apostle knew that disunity and contention are contrary to the presence of the Holy Ghost. Rather than risk offending the Spirit, he acquiesced. Yes, the stake president should have been more attuned to the preferences of the Apostle. But the Apostle demonstrated an important priesthood principle: Whether in the home or in the Church, unity is necessary in order for the Spirit to be present.

NOTE

1. Bruce C. Hafen. *A Disciple's Life: The Biography of Neal A. Maxwell* (2002), 454.

Chapter 22

PRINCIPLE #14
A PRIESTHOOD HOLDER GIVES
AND RECEIVES CORRECTION

Reproving . . . when moved upon by the Holy Ghost . . .
—DOCTRINE AND COVENANTS 121:43

Priesthood holders may be called on to correct behavior and admonish repentance. Both giving and receiving correction are
aspects of the doctrine of the priesthood. Giving correction may be
uncomfortable but should not be avoided. President Boyd K. Packer,
in training meetings with General Authorities and Area Seventies,
repeatedly said: "When a man who carries responsibility does not
correct when necessary, he is only thinking of himself."

The Prophet Joseph Smith stated the principle as follows: "I frequently rebuke and admonish my brethren, and that because I love
them, not because I wish to incur their displeasure, or mar their
happiness. . . . But these rebukes and admonitions become necessary . . . for their temporal as well as spiritual welfare. They actually
constitute a part of the duties of my station and calling."[1]

The Lord requires priesthood holders who are called to lead to perform this responsibility for the sake of the Church and for the sake of individual members. Thus, this responsibility may be part of the duty and station in some priesthood callings and should not be avoided. The Lord told Ezekiel: "So thou, O son of man, I have set thee a watchman unto the house of Israel; therefore thou shalt hear the word at my mouth, and warn them from me. When I say unto the wicked, O wicked man, thou shalt surely die; if thou dost not speak to warn the wicked from his way, that wicked man shall die in his iniquity; but his blood will I require at thine hand" (Ezekiel 33:7–8).

Similarly, Jacob and Joseph, the last-born sons of Lehi, understood this responsibility. Jacob writes: "And we did magnify our office unto the Lord, taking upon us the responsibility, answering the sins of the people upon our own heads if we did not teach them the word of God with all diligence; wherefore, by laboring with our might their blood might not come upon our garments; otherwise their blood would come upon our garments, and we would not be found spotless at the last day" (Jacob 1:19).

Like many priesthood principles, correcting others in the Lord's way can be learned. The Lord described this principle when he instructed Joseph Smith how to correct his brethren: "Reproving betimes with sharpness, when moved upon by the Holy Ghost; and then showing forth afterwards an increase of love toward him whom thou hast reproved, lest he esteem thee to be his enemy; that he may know that thy faithfulness is stronger than the cords of death" (Doctrine and Covenants 121:43–44).

In this verse, "reproving" simply means correcting. "Betimes" means early on, right away, or soon. "Sharpness" means clarity. The Holy Ghost must be present for "sharpness" not to be offensive.

Correction is best received when an individual understands expectations for the task at hand. If the priesthood holder delegating the assignment has not delegated clearly, he cannot expect the task to be completed correctly. A poor performance can often be attributed to poor instructions. Thorough instructions, expectations, and reporting accountability need to be specified as a task is assigned. If not, "reproving betimes with sharpness" will seem arbitrary and capricious. President Thomas S. Monson has said: "The secret to motivating is not criticism; rather is it praise for what is done right and gentle guidance for what needs correction. I know of no one who welcomes criticism—constructive or otherwise."[2]

The Savior's example of giving correction is instructive. It was never crushing. It often called for self-introspection. He often corrected people by asking probing questions, prompting the listeners to do their own soul searching. Priesthood holders should ask themselves how they can give needed correction without eroding people's confidence in their capacity to accomplish the task.

If giving correction is difficult, receiving correction may be even more difficult. A classic example of how a priesthood holder receives correction is given in an account of a public interaction between Joseph Smith and Brigham Young.

> In the presence of a rather large group of brethren, the Prophet severely chastised Brother Brigham for some failing in his duty. Everyone waited to see what Brigham's response would be. After all, Brigham, who later became known as the Lion of the Lord, was no shrinking violet by any means. Brigham slowly rose to his feet, and in words that truly reflected his character and his humility, he simply bowed his head and said, "Joseph, what do you want me to do?" The story goes that sobbing, Joseph ran from the podium, threw his arms around Brigham, and said in effect, "You passed, Brother Brigham, you passed."[3]

What test did Brigham pass? Brigham put aside his pride and self-justification to receive correction from his leader. It is usually not necessary or appropriate for priesthood leaders to develop tests for those whom they lead. The work in which we are engaged generally provides challenge enough. In this instance, Joseph felt to test Brigham, and from Brigham's response we learn a great lesson.

While we do not believe in the infallibility of Church leaders, there is great danger in assuming we are wiser than they. Joseph Smith stated it this way: "I will give you one of the Keys of the mysteries of the Kingdom. It is an eternal principle, that has existed with God from all eternity: That man who rises up to condemn others, finding fault with the Church, saying that they are out of the way, while he himself is righteous, then know assuredly, that that man is in the high road to apostasy; and if he does not repent, will apostatize, as God lives."[4]

A priesthood holder may find criticism unwelcome because he thinks it is unwarranted. The trap of "thinking ourselves wise" may be greatest for those who are educated or experienced (see 2 Nephi 9:28–29). However, the trap is real for everyone. How a priesthood holder receives correction determines how willing his leaders are to provide that counsel. We can either become defensive or we can welcome the correction as an opportunity to learn and improve. Parley P. Pratt, one of the original members of the Quorum of the Twelve, took the latter approach as he received counsel from Brigham Young.[5]

> During the exodus from Nauvoo in 1846, Parley was summoned from his camp to Brigham's camp in a letter of reproof. Despite being sick, Parley tried to get to Brigham's camp through difficult storms. While traveling, another letter from Brigham arrived, censuring Parley still more severely. When he finally reached Brigham's camp, Parley reports that

Brigham " . . . reproved and chastened us severely for several things . . . and here I would observe that, although my own motives were pure, so far as I could know my own heart, yet I thank God for this timely chastisement, I profited by it and it caused me to be more watchful and careful ever after."[6]

Parley could have reacted quite differently. But he used the counsel to improve himself. His commitment to receive counsel and learn from it is seen on another occasion. In 1847, another council was held and Parley "was highly censured and chastened by President [Brigham] Young and others." Parley reported: "In short, I was severely reproved and chastened. I no doubt deserved this chastisement; and I humbled myself, acknowledged my faults and errors, and asked forgiveness. . . . This school of experience made me more humble and careful in the future, and I think it was the means of making me a wiser and better man ever after."[7]

Growth and refinement come from repentance and humility. Though criticism may sting, it is often the mechanism for improvement.

On one occasion, I was called on to correct a mission president who had implemented an ambitious plan in his mission, which covered four different countries. He was motivated by his desire to fulfill his assignment and magnify his calling. Unfortunately, this plan involved spending money that had not been budgeted and allocated. By July of the year, the entire year's budget had been spent. A supplemental budget was approved. The Area Presidency met with the mission president and were direct in requesting that the mission president change his plans.

As I noticed the mission president's disappointment, I said, "I am sorry for the pain that we are causing by asking that you change direction." Interestingly, the mission president's countenance brightened. He smiled. Although there were tears in his eyes, he said very clearly, "Oh, Elder Renlund, there is no pain in being obedient, there is only joy." Thereafter, the mission president found ways to stay within his budget and still accomplish the work. He demonstrated his greatness of soul and his capability to accept correction.

The doctrine of the priesthood teaches the priesthood holder that he can learn from both giving and receiving correction. He should never shirk or shrink from either. But the key to both is love. Without love, giving correction may be viewed as mean-spirited. Without love for the Lord and His servants, the one receiving correction may take offense. A priesthood holder demonstrates his understanding of the doctrine of the priesthood when he learns these precepts.

NOTES

1. Joseph Smith, *History of the Church of Jesus Christ of Latter-day Saints,* 7 vols. (1932–51), 2:478.

2. Thomas S. Monson, remarks in department head meeting, August 4, 2006.

3. Truman G. Madsen, "Hugh B. Brown—Youthful Veteran," *New Era,* April 1976; see also Richard C. Edgley, "The Empowerment of Humility," *Ensign,* November 2003.

4. *Teachings of Presidents of the Church: Joseph Smith* (2007), 318.

5. Parley P. Pratt sacrificed much for the Church. He and Brigham Young were called as Apostles at the same time. Brigham was senior to Parley because he was older. After the martyrdom of Joseph and Hyrum Smith, Parley helped keep the Church together until other Apostles, including Brigham, could arrive in Nauvoo.

6. Parley P. Pratt, *Autobiography of Parley P. Pratt* (1938), 304–7.

7. Ibid., 330–31.

Chapter 23

Principle #15

A Priesthood Holder Judges Righteously

Ye shall be judges of this people.

—3 NEPHI 27:27

Priesthood holders may be asked to be judges in Israel. While not all are called to serve in these capacities, the priesthood principle of judging righteously is part of the doctrine of the priesthood. Fortunately, judges in Israel today are not required to judge medical matters, as did priests anciently. But they do need to be wise and use all their faculties to fulfill their duties correctly, as the following account illustrates.

As Israel wandered in the wilderness, an infectious disease called leprosy was of concern to the safe movement of a large camp of people. The Lord directed that if a suspect skin lesion were noted, the Israelite was quarantined and the priest assessed it over the course of two weeks. If the lesion "be deeper than the skin," it was diagnosed as leprosy, and the individual was permanently segregated from the congregation. On the other hand, if the "spot . . . be not deeper than the skin,"—in other words, if the lesion remained superficial—the quarantine ended (see Leviticus 13). A Talmudic scholar who wrote a commentary for Leviticus 13 suggested, "A one-eyed priest shall not judge cases of impurity."[1] Without binocular vision, a judge in Israel would have had difficulty determining whether the skin lesion was deep or superficial.

When called on to judge, a priesthood holder must metaphorically have both eyes open. Judging a person's soul is much harder than diagnosing leprosy. This weighty responsibility of judging falls to bishops and stake presidents and their counselors. Ecclesiastical judgments assess the worthiness of a member for ordinances and callings. Additionally, ecclesiastical judgments are used to help transgressors repent, to protect innocent victims, and to safeguard the Church.

The priesthood holder must use good judgment. Unfortunately, the conferral of priesthood does not automatically confer good judgment. Good judgment is either brought to the calling or acquired during the magnifying of it. A priesthood holder needs to know when he should praise and encourage, calm and pacify, exhort and commit, or supplicate and persuade. A priesthood holder who exhorts when he should instead offer praise makes an error in judgment. The Holy Ghost will help, but it is difficult for the Holy Ghost to work with a priesthood holder who is insensitive to others' feelings or oblivious to circumstances.

Righteous judging requires a priesthood holder to be certain of the details of specific circumstances and the correct course of action. He should be honest with himself and others. If he is uncertain, he should be willing to acknowledge it and say, "I don't know." He can learn from Alma, who said: "Now these mysteries are not yet fully made known unto me; therefore I shall forbear" (Alma 37:11).

Priesthood leaders make mistakes when they make up answers or invent explanations that have not been revealed by God.

Priesthood leaders also manifest bad judgment when they continue pursuing a path that is obviously wrong, perhaps settling for minor course corrections when a complete change of direction is needed. Elder Merlin R. Lybbert, Sister Renlund's father, said that such a course violates the "First Rule of Holes": "When you're in one, stop digging!"

A priesthood holder who evaluates his actions, motives, and direction regularly and objectively will grow in his capacity to exercise good judgment. This is particularly true in counseling individuals regarding the timing of a temple endowment or a patriarchal blessing, or in responding to emotional challenges. Good judgment often means talking less and listening more. As Philippe de Commynes said, « *Je me suis souvent repenti d'avoir parlé, mais jamais de m'être tu.* » Or, as we would say in English, "I have often regretted having spoken, but never having kept silent."

A priesthood holder performs a great service by listening and allowing the Holy Ghost time to communicate. Good judgment is acquired over time as a priesthood holder abides by the doctrine of the priesthood and listens to the Holy Ghost.

The Savior's statement, "Judge not, that ye be not judged" (Matthew 7:1), may make a priesthood holder hesitant to judge others because His statement is followed by a caution, "For with what judgment ye judge, ye shall be judged: and with what measure ye mete, it shall be measured to you again" (Matthew 7:2).

Yet, priesthood leaders are under mandate to render judgment. The Joseph Smith Translation of the Bible offers clarity on this passage: "Now these are the words which Jesus taught his disciples that they should say unto the people. Judge not unrighteously, that ye be not judged; but judge righteous judgment" (JST, Matthew 7:1–2).

Jesus did not prohibit judging others; rather, He enjoined judging righteously.

The Savior told His disciples in the Americas the kind of judges they should be: "And know ye that ye shall be judges of this people, according to the judgment which I shall give unto you, which shall be just. Therefore, what manner of men ought ye to be? Verily I say unto you, even as I am" (3 Nephi 27:27).

How are priesthood holders today to judge? They are to render judgment by following the Savior's perfect example. They judge as He would. To give His kind of judgment requires spiritual insight, experience, and wisdom. Paul told Timothy that a judge in Israel, a bishop, should "not [be] a novice, lest being lifted up with pride he fall into the condemnation of the devil" (1 Timothy 3:6).

Judging righteously requires more than following directions in a handbook. Judging in the Lord's way requires relying on every aspect of the doctrine of the priesthood, especially Christlike virtues.

Priesthood leaders may be called on to help a transgressor repent. The Lord provided a framework for Alma to use in judging and helping transgressors. The Savior said:

> For behold, this is my church; whosoever is baptized shall be baptized unto repentance. And whomsoever ye receive shall believe in my name; and him will I freely forgive.
>
> For it is I that taketh upon me the sins of the world; for it is I that hath created them; and it is I that granteth unto him that believeth unto the end a place at my right hand. . . .
>
> Therefore I say unto you, Go; and whosoever transgresseth against me, him shall ye judge according to the sins which he has committed; and *if he confess his sins before thee and me, and repenteth in the sincerity of his heart, him shall ye forgive, and I will forgive him also.*

Yea, and as often as my people repent will I forgive them their trespasses against me. . . .

Now I say unto you, Go; and whosoever will not repent of his sins the same shall not be numbered among my people; and this shall be observed from this time forward. (Mosiah 26:22–23, 29–30, 32; emphasis added)

The framework for judging and helping transgressors includes these truths:

- This is the Lord's Church; He has the right to forgive sin.
- The Lord forgives all who are baptized unto repentance.
- Those who confess sins to a priesthood leader and to God, and who repent, should be forgiven by the Church and will be forgiven by God.
- As often as people repent, God will forgive them.
- Those who fail to repent should not be numbered among the Church.

The role of a priesthood leader in judging transgressors is to help the transgressor repent and receive forgiveness from God. The priesthood leader cannot ignore sinful behavior. Making excuses for an individual does not help that person repent.

God's love for the transgressor is divine and infinite.[2] A priesthood holder should immediately convey His love and offer positive reinforcement for transgressors who come before him. The leader should suppress any surprise or disbelief as a member confesses his or her actions. The transgressor's confession may be the first good decision he or she has made in a long time. The priesthood leader should consider thanking the individual for having the confidence and faith to repent.

The worth of a soul is great in the eyes of God (see Doctrine and Covenants 18:10). How great? As related in a story by President Thomas S. Monson, his former stake president, President Paul C.

Child, once asked those attending a priesthood leadership meeting, "Who can tell me the worth of a human soul?" President Child then called on an unsuspecting elders quorum president, who hesitantly asked that President Child repeat the question. The elders quorum president thought for a moment and then said, "The worth of a human soul is its capacity to become as God." As President Child passed President Monson on the way back to the podium, President Monson heard President Child utter, "a profound reply; a profound reply."[3]

Given the great worth of souls, a priesthood holder should take the time necessary to help individuals through the repentance process. He should not rush the one who is confessing, nor should he be in a hurry to resolve the matter. With rare exception, matters typically being confessed do not require immediate resolution. A short delay may cause angst in the transgressor, but the priesthood leader may need time to think about the matter and seek inspiration. He may need to study the scriptures and handbooks for help.

In complicated matters, a bishop or stake president may wish to discuss an issue or situation with his counselors. The priesthood leader should first take care to obtain permission to divulge the transgressor's name or circumstances. Priesthood holders should be very wary of the "do you have a minute" type of confessions in which the transgressor is demanding a quick decision as to outcome. A wise priesthood leader will not be pressured for a decision until he has received input from those who have been hurt by the transgressions.

Taking time ensures that all the "dirty laundry" is out on the table. Some sins are accompanied by other sins. Having the whole picture of the transgression and any associated transgressions leads to correct assessment. Take time to teach correct doctrine, particularly regarding the Atonement of Jesus Christ. Teach that it is the

Savior who forgives, who eventually judges, and not the priesthood leader.

A judge in Israel has an awesome opportunity to help a transgressor partake of the Atonement. Helping a member through the repentance process may be the most important part of his priesthood service. When he approaches this responsibility with love for the transgressor, he can help the transgressor feel the Savior's love. Because a priesthood leader represents the Savior in judging others, he must ensure that his judgment is accompanied by the Holy Ghost.

NOTES

1. Harold S. Kushner, *Overcoming Life's Disappointments* (2006), 38–39.

2. See Russell M. Nelson, "Divine Love," *Ensign,* February 2003.

3. Thomas S. Monson, *A Prophet's Voice: Messages from Thomas S. Monson* (2012), 291–92.

Chapter 24

Conclusion

They do not learn this one lesson . . .
—DOCTRINE AND COVENANTS 121:35

The doctrine of the priesthood includes the set of principles that govern the use of God's power and authority. Collectively, these principles are encapsulated by the principles of righteousness. The critical lesson that a priesthood holder must learn is that the priesthood conferred upon him is inseparably connected with God's total priesthood power and authority, also called the powers of heaven.

"The rights of the priesthood are inseparably connected with the powers of heaven, and . . . the powers of heaven cannot be controlled nor handled only upon the principles of righteousness" (Doctrine and Covenants 121:36).

Because of their inseparable connection, neither God's total priesthood power and authority nor that portion of God's authority and power delegated to man on earth through priesthood ordination can be "controlled" or "handled" except by using "principles of righteousness." In other words, the control of God's power and authority occurs only in accord with the doctrine of the priesthood. Over time, as the doctrine of the priesthood distills on the priesthood holder's soul as dews from heaven, and unrighteousness is purged from him, his priesthood power can be . . . well, explosive.

Consider one last scientific analogy.[1] Until the middle of the nineteenth century, the most powerful explosive material known in the world was black powder. A mixture of charcoal, sulfur, and potassium nitrate, black powder had been around for many centuries. While it could propel musket or cannon balls and was relatively stable and safe, it was not powerful enough for other desirable tasks, such as for most mining applications.

In 1847, a chemist named Ascanio Sobrero, working at a university in Italy, made a completely new explosive material with amazing properties. Instead of being a mixture of several different compounds, it was a single pure chemical compound that was about 1,000 times more powerful than black powder. This opened a whole range of new applications: the new explosive could shatter rock with great efficiency. This material was named nitroglycerin.

Unfortunately, nitroglycerin is very unstable. If you drop a bottle of it from a small height, it will blow up. If it gets too hot, it will blow up. If it gets too cold and forms crystals, it will blow up. In fact, if you put it on a shelf in a cool, dark room and leave it alone, it will eventually blow up. If it could safely be deployed to where it was needed, mining and road construction, especially in mountainous areas, would be much easier. But after many costly and fatal accidents involving nitroglycerin, most U.S. states and European countries banned its transportation or even its manufacture. It was inherently unstable.

A Swedish scientist was determined to find a way for nitroglycerin to be used safely. He tried mixing it or absorbing it into various materials in the hopes of stabilizing this powerful explosive without affecting its power. He eventually found a suitable stabilizing material. A very porous, claylike material known as kieselguhr or diatomaceous earth could act like a rigid wick to absorb liquid nitroglycerin.[2] The kieselguhr could be cut into "sticks" of suitable size. Once the nitroglycerin was absorbed into the stick, it was much more stable. It could be safely stored and transported. The inherent power in nitroglycerin was now usable.

The scientist who discovered the stabilization process was Alfred Nobel, and he named his new material "dynamite." Dynamite was created by putting two known materials together, nitroglycerin and kieselguhr. It is not an exaggeration to say that dynamite changed the world and made Alfred Nobel a very wealthy man. The same could not be said for Ascanio Sobrero, the scientist who first synthesized nitroglycerin.

No one in their right mind entrusted nitroglycerin to non-experts. Even experts had to be cautious. But when nitroglycerin was combined with kieselguhr, miners, road-construction workers, and others could use it safely.

Like nitroglycerin, priesthood power can only be controlled or handled with great care. It is not an exaggeration to say that the doctrine of the priesthood—principles of righteousness plus priesthood power—can change the world. It already has. A righteous man, Joseph Smith, doing the best he could, exercised his priesthood authority and was the instrument God used to restore all His saving ordinances to earth. Righteous men who received a portion of God's authority to act in His name left home and family to spread the good news of the gospel of Jesus Christ. They changed the world.

Righteous men who accept and honor their priesthood covenants continue to change the world for themselves and their families. Righteous men who accept and honor their priesthood covenants by accepting priesthood responsibilities change their wards and stakes. Righteous men who accept and honor their priesthood covenants and bear witness to others change the world one soul at a time. Righteous priesthood holders today are changing the world so that Jesus Christ will come again in power and glory. Righteousness and priesthood are an explosive combination.

NOTES

1. See A. P. Cartwright, *The Dynamite Company: The Story of African Explosives and Chemical Industries Limited* (1964); H. Schück and R. Sohlman, *The Life of Alfred Nobel* (1929); Thomas Hellberg and Lars Magnus Jansson, *Alfred Nobel,* rev. ed. (1986).

2. Kieselguhr does have another modern-day usage: as kitty litter. It very efficiently absorbs cat urine. But, by itself, it is not very valuable.

CHAPTER SUMMARIES

INTRODUCTION: *Foundations and Doctrine of the Priesthood*

The doctrine of the priesthood includes a set of principles governing the use of the priesthood. To properly exercise priesthood authority and understand the principles of righteousness, one must understand the foundational aspects of priesthood authority and power. The exercise of the priesthood must be coupled with a genuine love of all mankind. Abiding by this set of principles strengthens one's assurance, belief, and trust in God. Properly exercising priesthood authority over time becomes more natural.

CHAPTER 1: *The Priesthood*

The term *priesthood* is used in two ways. The first is to describe the power and authority of God. The second is to describe the power and authority that God gives to ordained priesthood holders on earth to act in all things necessary for the salvation of God's children. God has not delegated all of His priesthood power and authority to men on earth. Those who are not ordained to the priesthood can still be blessed by God's priesthood power and authority. However, it is only through the Atonement of Jesus Christ and by obedience to the ordinances of the priesthood, administered through delegated priesthood keys, that all mankind may be saved (see Articles of Faith 1:3). God determines who receives ordination to priesthood office. The priesthood achieves its highest aims in the family where the father presides in righteousness and uses his priesthood to bless his family.

CHAPTER 2: *Priesthood Offices and Keys*

The conferral of the Aaronic and Melchizedek Priesthoods is associated with priesthood offices and keys. The offices of deacon, teacher, priest, and bishop pertain to the Aaronic Priesthood. The offices of elder, high priest, patriarch, Seventy, and Apostle pertain to the Melchizedek Priesthood. Some priesthood keys are given to all priesthood holders, and some priesthood keys are given only to leaders. Except in the case of Apostles, priesthood keys of leadership are held only temporarily and are relinquished upon a release. Priesthood keys are the mechanism by which the Lord organizes His priesthood on earth. A man with priesthood keys has specific and special responsibilities in addition to those that accompany his ordination to an office in the priesthood.

CHAPTER 3: *Priesthood Keys and the Holy Apostleship*

Upon being ordained an Apostle and set apart as a member of the Quorum of the Twelve, a man receives every right, gift, authority, and priesthood key that has been conferred in this dispensation. These include the keys of prophet, seer, and revelator and are intrinsic to the office. These keys are held for life, not temporarily. Even though all Apostles hold all priesthood keys, only the President of the Church, the senior Apostle, is authorized to exercise them all. He delegates authority by giving or authorizing the use of priesthood keys by others.

CHAPTER 4: *The Priesthood Blesses the Priesthood Holder*

The priesthood blesses individuals who hold it. The priesthood holder is blessed with greater happiness, peace and rest, righteousness, knowledge, and family blessings. He becomes a joint-heir with Jesus Christ to all that Heavenly Father has. These blessings are the greatest the Lord can promise.

CHAPTER 5: *The Priesthood Blesses Others*

The primary purpose of the priesthood is to bless others. The priesthood is tasked with making available to each man and woman the saving and exalting ordinances and associated covenants, which when kept invite all the blessings of the Savior's atoning sacrifice into their lives. Through His Atonement, the bondage of sin may be removed. The priesthood holder can then stand with the Savior in fulfilling His mission.

CHAPTER 6: *Oaths and Covenants*

Oaths and covenants are pledges and vows that guarantee the behavior of the participant. Because a covenant is a pledge of self, it defines a man. He should be totally committed to fulfilling it. Breaking the oath or the vow diminishes the man. His very soul is jeopardized. The priesthood covenant is an agreement between God and man. God in his good pleasure fixes the terms, which man accepts.

CHAPTER 7: *The Oath and Covenant of the Priesthood*

The two priesthoods in the Church, the Aaronic and Melchizedek Priesthoods, are both associated with covenants. Aaronic Priesthood holders covenant to be free from iniquity, lead others from iniquity, help individuals become reconciled to God, and prepare to receive the Melchizedek Priesthood. God promises hope, forgiveness, the ministering of angels, and keys for the preparatory gospel. Melchizedek Priesthood holders covenant to magnify their callings by keeping commandments associated with the covenant. God then promises, with an oath, that Melchizedek Priesthood holders will become heirs to the blessings of Abraham, be sanctified by the Spirit to the renewing of their bodies, and become joint-heirs with Jesus Christ to Heavenly Father's kingdom.

CHAPTER 8: *Commandments of the Melchizedek Priesthood Covenant*

A priesthood holder magnifies his calling in the priesthood by keeping the commandments of the Melchizedek Priesthood covenant. The first commandment is to pay attention to and obey God's word. God's word comes from scriptures, living prophets, handbooks, file leaders, and the Holy Ghost. The second commandment is to take the testimony of the Savior to all the world. Doing so helps the priesthood holder accomplish God's work and assists him in obtaining his own salvation. The third commandment is to not boast but to give glory to God for miracles that occur during the priesthood holder's ministry. The fourth commandment is to become a friend to the Savior. As a priesthood holder does so, the Savior provides him all the support he needs to accomplish the work of salvation.

CHAPTER 9: *Principle #1—The Rights of the Priesthood Are Governed by Principles of Righteousness*

Because the rights of the priesthood are connected to the powers of heaven, the priesthood can be used only in righteousness. Although no priesthood holder is perfect, the priesthood cannot be used for unrighteous pursuits. An imperfect man can exercise the priesthood in accordance with correct principles with good effect, but even a perfect man cannot exercise the priesthood for improper purposes.

CHAPTER 10: *Principle #2—The Proper Exercise of Priesthood Is Learned*

The proper exercise of priesthood must be learned. It is not instinctive or natural. Patterns in the world are not the correct models to follow. Rather, the proper exercise of priesthood is learned by following the Savior's example and the example of other experienced priesthood holders.

CHAPTER 11: *Principle #3—A Calling in the Priesthood Is a Calling to Serve*

Intrinsic to holding the priesthood is the responsibility to serve others. A priesthood holder follows the Savior's example and seeks to serve others rather than to be served. The priesthood holder focuses on ministering rather than on efficiency. He always recognizes that people are far more important than any program or task.

CHAPTER 12: *Principle #4—A Priesthood Holder Recognizes and Follows Righteous Patterns*

Recognizing and abiding by the Lord's patterns in priesthood service helps priesthood holders avoid making mistakes. For a priesthood holder to trust another's judgment, he should be able to observe that an individual is obedient, has complied with the ordinances of the gospel, has a contrite spirit, speaks in an edifying manner, is clearly influenced by God, and is not self-congratulatory. Others will be edified by his speech. Patterns can be learned by observing experienced priesthood holders as they exercise their priesthood.

CHAPTER 13: *Principle #5—A Priesthood Holder's Identity Becomes Christlike*

A priesthood holder strives to become a disciple of Jesus Christ and then helps others become the Savior's disciples. A priesthood holder sees all men and women as children of God. A priesthood holder puts his discipleship before his own identity. He becomes all things to all people so that he may help more come unto Christ.

CHAPTER 14: *Principle #6—Priesthood Power and Influence Are Maintained Using Christlike Attributes*

A priesthood holder is most effective using Christlike attributes. He must be gentle, meek, loving, kind, virtuous, temperate, patient, godly, and charitable in his service. Through these attributes, his priesthood authority, power, and influence are maintained. This is the way he invites all to come unto Christ.

CHAPTER 15: *Principle #7—A Priesthood Holder Must Be Willing to Be Presided Over*

A priesthood holder is not fit to preside over others until he can submit sufficiently to those who preside over him. Though priesthood leaders are not infallible, a priesthood holder sustains those who preside over him. Priesthood holders demonstrate their support with their confidence, faith, and prayers.

CHAPTER 16: *Principle #8—A Priesthood Holder Serves Where Called*

In contrast to individuals who ambitiously seek leadership positions for personal reasons, a priesthood holder serves where he is called. Priesthood leaders hold their callings for a season and then are released. Thanks for priesthood service comes from the Lord.

CHAPTER 17: *Principle #9—A Priesthood Holder Fulfills His Duty*

A priesthood holder must first learn and then do his duty. Fulfilling one's duty not only helps accomplish an important task but also prevents adverse consequences from occurring. As a priesthood holder performs his duty, he has a right to feel pleased, but should not be satisfied until all of God's purposes are accomplished.

CHAPTER 18: *Principle #10—A Priesthood Holder Delegates and Accepts Delegated Responsibility*

Priesthood holders teach correct principles and let people govern themselves. They also delegate and accept assignments. Delegation blesses both the one who delegates and the one to whom a task is delegated. The pattern established in Christ's day is applicable today: the experienced people work alongside the less experienced to build up the Church for the Savior. Working synergistically increases the rate at which the Church is established.

CHAPTER 19: *Principle #11—A Priesthood Holder Works Effectively in Councils*

The Church is governed through councils and committees. Priesthood holders participate and preside in these meetings. They are mindful that Church councils and committees follow a pattern for governing that is distinct in the world today. Priesthood holders work to create a revelatory experience by understanding goals, roles, preparation, agendas, etiquette, assignments, statistics, decision making, and outcomes.

CHAPTER 20: *Principle #12—A Priesthood Holder Sees Himself as Equal with Others*

A priesthood holder understands that he is valued no more than any other of God's children. This understanding facilitates and informs his service. He recognizes that the work of each member is vital and valued in the work of the Lord.

CHAPTER 21: *Principle #13—A Priesthood Holder Works in Unity*

Priesthood holders understand that the Holy Ghost will only be part of the work when unity exists. Priesthood holders must be righteous, holy, humble, patient, meek, virtuous, and kind. Achieving unity comes at a cost, and disunity leaves priesthood holders weak. Achieving unity requires submission of ego, assuming the best intent of others, and taking the time to counsel together. The one who presides has the greater responsibility to ensure that unity is achieved.

CHAPTER 22: *Principle #14—A Priesthood Holder Gives and Receives Correction*

Priesthood holders may hold priesthood offices that involve a duty to give correction to others. Correction must be given timely, specifically, and with love. Priesthood holders must also be willing to accept correction, putting aside pride and self-justification.

CHAPTER 23: *Principle #15—A Priesthood Holder Judges Righteously*

Priesthood holders who are called to be "judges in Israel" are given a weighty responsibility to certify worthiness for ordinances and help Heavenly Father's children repent. In these matters, a priesthood holder must exercise good judgment. A priesthood holder must recognize that this is the Lord's Church; it is the Lord who forgives all who are baptized unto repentance. Those who confess sins should be accepted by the Church and will be forgiven by God. A priesthood holder should realize that as often as people repent, God will forgive them.

INDEX

conferral and unauthorized use of, 24n6; purpose of, 42–43, 51, 53; blesses priesthood holder, 42–49; blesses others, 50–55; repentance and restoration of, 53–54; oath and covenant of, 60–72, 73–74nn4,5, 75; structure of, 62–63; rights of, governed by principles of righteousness, 89–92; governed by eternal laws, 90–92; as learned, 93–95; and service, 96–103; seeking, 128–29; inseparably connected with powers of heaven, 171. *See also* Foundations of the priesthood; Principles of the priesthood

Priesthood authority: restrictions on, 1–2; impairment of, 3; proper exercise of, 3, 4, 6–7; of God, 12–15; unknown aspects of, 16–18; women and, 18–21; expression of, in family, 21–23; maintained through Christlike attributes, 115–18

Priesthood blessings, 138–39, 140–41

Priesthood influence, maintained through Christlike attributes, 115–18

Priesthood keys: knowledge concerning, 15–16; uses of term, 26–27; and apostleship,

28–39; authority to exercise, 40n14

Priesthood offices, 25–26

Priesthood ordination, restrictions on, 16–21

Priesthood power: exercise of, 2, 4, 173–74; of God, 12–15; unknown aspects of, 16–18; exercised by women, 18–21; expression of, in family, 21–23; maintained through Christlike attributes, 115–18; seeking, 128–29

Priesthood quorums, 50

Prince of peace, 48

Principles of the priesthood, 3–4; regarding righteousness and rights of priesthood, 89–92; regarding learning priesthood, 93–95; regarding callings, 96–103, 126–30; regarding righteous patterns, 104–9; regarding Christlike identity, 110–14; regarding priesthood power and influence, 115–18; regarding presiding authority, 119–25; regarding fulfilling duty, 131–34; regarding delegation, 135–41; regarding councils, 142–49; regarding equality, 150–52; regarding unity, 153–57; regarding correction, 158–63; regarding righteous judgment, 164–70

Brigham Young, 160–61; on criticizing Church leaders, 161
Smith, Joseph F., 115–16, 119
Smith, Joseph Fielding, 73n4
Smith, William, 39n2
Snow, Lorenzo, 36
Sobrero, Ascanio, 172, 173
Soul, worth of, 168–69
Spirit, contrite, 106
Spiritual knowledge, 45–46
Statistics, 147
Sticks, priesthood compared to, 120–21
Submission, to presiding authority, 119–25
Sweden, 90–91
Synergy, 139–40

Talmage, James E., 123
Taylor, John, 134
Teaching by more experienced priesthood holders, 137–39
Temple sealing, 20, 21
Thanks, for priesthood service, 130
Thomas, Brother, 138
Thorvaldsen, Bertel, 29

Transgressors, judging and helping, 167–70

Unanimity, 37–38, 41n17. *See also* Unity
Unintended patterns, 108–9
Unity, 153–57. *See also* Unanimity
Unrighteous dominion, 93, 94

Vasa, 90–91

Watchtower, 155–56
Will of God, 38–39, 120
Women, priesthood and, 18–21
Woodruff, Wilford, 30–31
Word of God, commandment to heed, 76–79
Work of God, 107–8
Worth: of priesthood holders, 150–52; of souls, 168–69

Yankton Sioux, 56–57
Young, Brigham, 12–13, 23–24n3, 122–23, 160–62

Zarahemla, 22–23, 57
Zion, redemption of, 155–56
Zoram, 57